THE WORD™ BOOK

A Program to Build
Expressive Vocabulary and Semantic Skills

Rosemary Huisingh
Mark Barrett
Linda Zachman
Carolyn Blagden
Jane Orman

LinguiSystems, Inc.
00 4th Avenue
ast Moline, IL 61244

Problem / Skill Area:	Vocabulary
Developmental Age:	7 thru 12 years
Interest Level:	1st thru 8th grade

800-PRO IDEA

ISBN# 1-55999-082-1

About the Authors

Rosemary, Mark and Linda, co-owners of LinguiSystems, are speech-language clinicians who have authored many popular, practical programs based on their extensive clinical experience and their love of language. Their publications include the *Manual of Exercises for Expressive Reasoning (MEER)*, *Activities for Children Involving Everyday Vocabulary (ACHIEV)*, *Teaching Vocabulary*, the *Test Of Problem Solving (TOPS)*, *The WORD Test*, *Assessing Semantic Skills through Everyday Themes (ASSET)*, and others.

Carolyn and Jane are also publishing speech-language clinicians at LinguiSystems. They have co-authored several programs with Rosemary, Mark, and Linda, including *Teaching Vocabulary Worksheets*, *Thinking To Go*, *Blooming Language Arts*, and *Ready, Set, Grammar*!

September 1988

We welcome your comments on *The Word Book* and other LinguiSystems products. Please send your comments to:

Carolyn Blagden
Editorial Manager
LinguiSystems, Inc.
3100 4th Avenue
East Moline, IL 61244

Table of Contents

Associations

Synonyms

Semantic
Absurdities

Antonyms

Definitions

Multiple
Definitions

Introduction

Thousands of you have used *The WORD Test* to evaluate the vocabulary and semantic skills of your language-delayed students aged seven and older. You've told us *The WORD Test* helps you identify areas of strength and weakness and, more importantly, plan therapy. Now, LinguiSystems has developed *The WORD Kit,* a complete therapy program you can use to teach your students the vocabulary and semantic skills they need. We know you'll find *The WORD Kit* as beneficial as *The WORD Test*!

Many language-delayed children learn vocabulary and semantic rules differently from their peers. They often haven't developed knowledge of the semantic features of words, so they can't identify words with similar meanings or those that "go together." These students have trouble understanding humor and figurative language. Because of their limited understanding of words and word meanings, they do not perform well on vocabulary tasks involving word relationships.

The WORD Kit is designed to teach your students to think about words and their relationships. They will learn that the semantic features of both a word and its synonym are almost identical. They will also learn that one critical feature of a target word and its antonym must be reversed. As your students understand the meanings of words and the relationships between key words in a sentence, they will develop a richer understanding and use of language.

The six sections of each component in the *The WORD Kit* correspond to the six tasks of *The WORD Test*:

- Associations
- Synonyms
- Semantic Absurdities
- Antonyms
- Definitions
- Multiple Definitions

The WORD Book

The WORD Book includes 260 pages of reproducible worksheets featuring the six vocabulary areas of *The WORD Kit*. The workbook activities include rebus stories, matching, crossword puzzles, multiple choice questions, sentence completion, and riddles — with lots of variety in between! Your students will truly enjoy working on their vocabulary and semantic skills in the multitude of formats provided, and they'll discover that learning can be a fascinating experience!

In addition to the activity pages, The WORD Book has an Answer Key and a Word List at the back. The Answer Key provides answers for worksheet activities where necessary. In some cases, more than one answer may be appropriate, so accept any reasonable responses. Vocabulary words used in the worksheets are listed alphabetically by grade level in the Word List for your reference.

The WORD Pictures

There are 300 picture cards in *The WORD Kit*, 50 for each of the six sections listed above. Each card has a picture (or pictures) on one side and vocabulary tasks on the other side. The picture cards are designed to increase your students' flexibility in using words. A variety of questions is provided for each target word on a card. You can use the cards alone for vocabulary training by asking the target question in the box at the top of each card, or by asking any combination of questions to learn even more about each vocabulary word. The WORD Pictures are also an integral part of The WORD Game.

The WORD Game

The WORD Game is a fast-moving, competitive game, with every question designed to increase your students' vocabulary and semantic skills in a fun, exciting way. Students use The WORD Pictures and WORD WATCH cards along with the game board and playing pieces to play The WORD Game. Complete instructions for The WORD Game are provided in the instruction manual. Your students will find The WORD Game a wonderful way to improve their vocabulary and semantic skills without considering it work!

General Instructions

The tasks in The WORD Pictures and The WORD Book are arranged by order of difficulty so you can concentrate on the ones most important for your students based on test results, parental and academic information,

and your own professional impressions. As your students progress through the materials, they will improve their ability to complete curriculum vocabulary tasks. Here are some "how to" tips for using the materials in your kit.

- Consider teaching across sections rather than completing all the activities for one vocabulary task before going on to another. The worksheets and picture cards are arranged in hierarchical order, so begin with those materials your students can successfully complete. When completing the activities, ask your students to explain how they arrived at their answers. For example, have them tell you why they matched opposite words as they did, how they decided that two words meant the same thing, or why a sentence didn't make sense. Then, you can send the worksheets home for carryover activities.

- Use the picture cards as flash cards or in other special games such as The WORD Game. We all know games should be fun, and The WORD Game definitely is! It will keep your students motivated to play again and again, and not become discouraged. You can also reproduce the picture cards for students to write their own questions for the pictures, then send them home for carryover activities. Your students will get hours of practice on their vocabulary and semantic skills with the help of these fun picture cards!

The blend of written and oral activities in *The WORD Kit* is designed to provide the kind of reinforcement and training your students need to grow more proficient in the use of language, while giving you maximum flexibility in teaching. Enjoy *The WORD Kit* as you have *The WORD Test* — and watch your students enjoy learning!

Associations

Children first learn to categorize words by class and function, then by the semantic features of size, shape, color, quality, and composition. As they grow and interact with their environment, children also learn how to subcategorize words. For example, they learn to classify vegetables into the sub-categories of vegetables that are green, grow underground, have skins, and so forth. They also learn that words can cross over into different categories, so that they understand that a bicycle can belong to the category "toy" as well as to the category "vehicle."

The language-delayed child often cannot identify an unrelated word that does not go with a group of related words. He doesn't recognize which attribute the related words share, or he can't identify the attribute the unrelated word does not possess that the others do. He has not developed knowledge of the identical semantic features of the related words, so he is not able to justify the exclusion of the unrelated word. For example, when asked to justify the exclusion of the word "Mary" from the group of words "Tom, Bill, John, Mary," the child might say, "Mary is a girl." The expected response is "The others are boys" or "Mary is not a boy." Although there are a variety of acceptable responses, the language-delayed child may need help in classifying according to a similar attribute or excluding because of a particular attribute.

Categorizing is one indication of a child's grasp of semantic attributes. Being able to categorize and subcategorize words means that the child is developing his knowledge of semantic features. This knowledge will help to increase his understanding of subject matter in the classroom and will enable him to participate more effectively in classroom discussions. These Associations worksheets emphasize categorizing words by semantic features in order to increase children's knowledge of identical semantic features and to teach reasoning about why words go together.

I'm Seeing Red!

Name _____

Look at the pictures below. Find the ones that go together because they're red. Then, color them red.

1.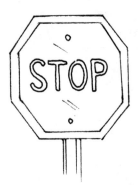

3.

4.

5.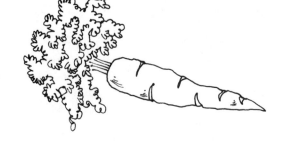

6.

7.

8.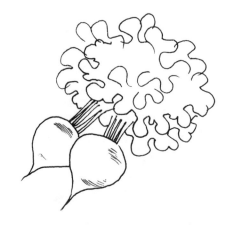

Now, name three more things that are red.

Furniture Sale!

The furniture store is having a sale! Look at the pictures below to see what they're selling. Then, draw a brown circle around each piece of furniture. Be careful! There is more than just furniture in this store!

1.

2.

3.

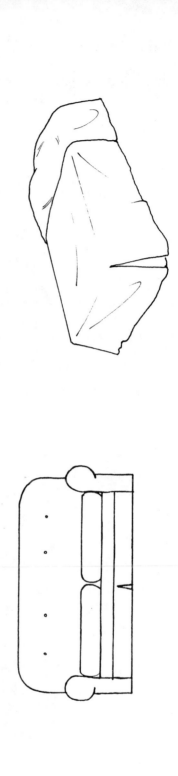

4.

5.

6.

Now, tell me which of the things above you could sleep on.

9

Home Sweet Home

Name _____

Look at these places where animals live. Then, look at the pictures of animals. Cut the animal pictures out and paste them in the places where they live. They don't like to be far from home!

1.

2.

3.

There's no place like home!

Shape Up

Name _____

Sometimes things go together because they're the same shape. Look at the pictures below. The pictures in each row have the same shape. Draw the shape of the pictures in the box at the end of each row. Then, name the shapes.

1.

2.

3.

Your answers are in good shape!

See the Light

Some things go together because they give us light so we can see. Draw a circle around each picture that gives us light.

1.

2.

3.

4. _____

5.

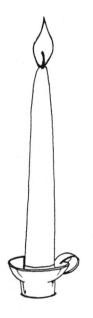

6.

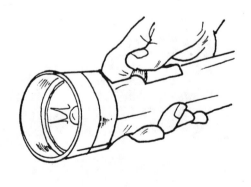

You're very bright!

Just Like Another

Draw a circle around all the pictures in each row that go with the first picture. Then, tell why they go together.

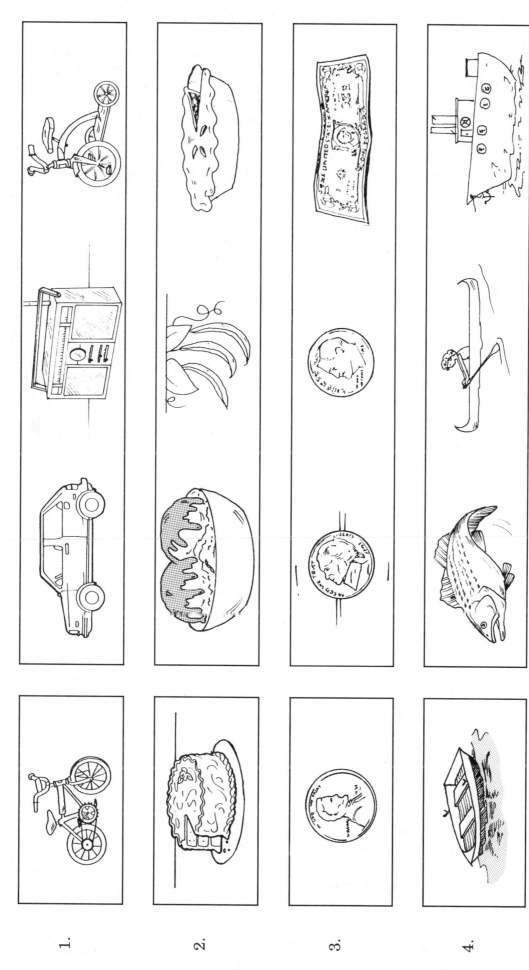

1.

2.

3.

4.

Now, name something else that could go in each row.

Animal Match

Name _____

Let's find out why these pictures go together. Draw a line to match each animal on the left to an animal on the right. Then, answer the questions below to find out why the animals go together.

1.

2.

3.

4.

5.

6.

7. All these animals could live on a _____ .

8. The animals in the first column are _____ .

9. The animals in the second column are _____ .

Do you have a pet? Tell me all about it!

14

Some Like It Hot

Name _____

Some things go together because of their temperature. Temperature is how hot or cold something is. Look at the thermometers below. One shows a cold temperature and the other shows a hot temperature. Circle each picture that's hot with a red crayon. Draw a blue line under each picture that's cold.

1.

2.

3.

4.

5.

6.

Your work is red hot!

How Are They Alike?

Draw a circle around all the pictures in each row that go with the first picture. Then, tell why they go together.

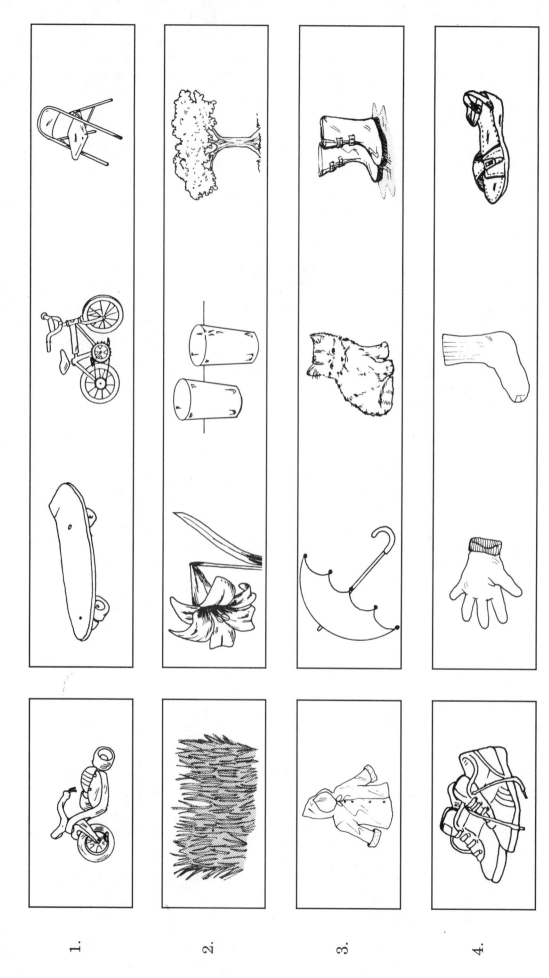

1.

2.

3.

4.

Two words that describe how you're doing are "great" and "super!"

Color Me True

Color all the pictures in each row that go together. Then, tell why they go together.

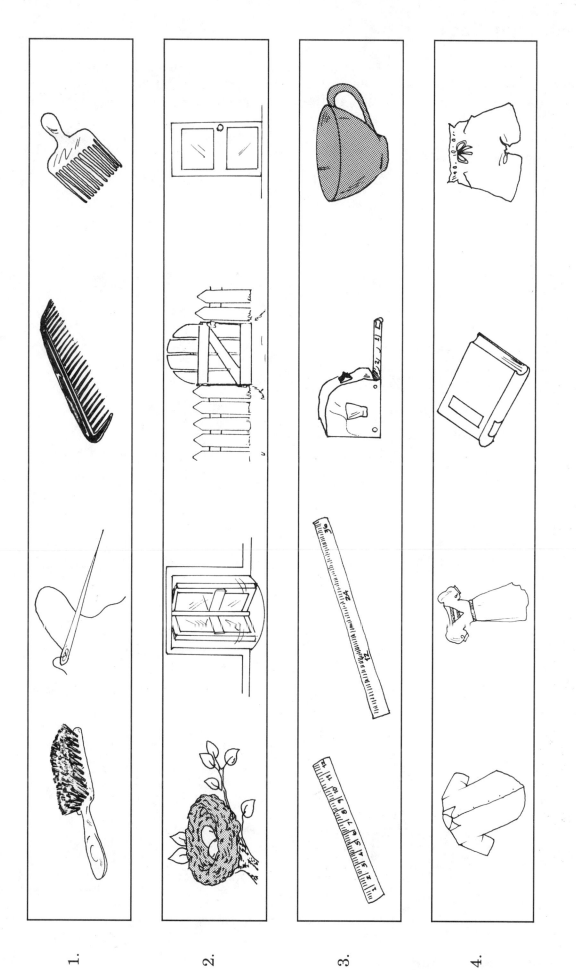

1.

2.

3.

4.

Can you tell me one more thing that goes with each row of pictures you colored?

17

Pack Your Bags

Name _____

Susan is packing her bags for a trip. She is taking three bags — one for clothes, one for snacks, and one for things to read. Help her finish packing by drawing a line from each picture to the bag it should go in. The sooner you finish, the sooner Susan can leave for her trip!

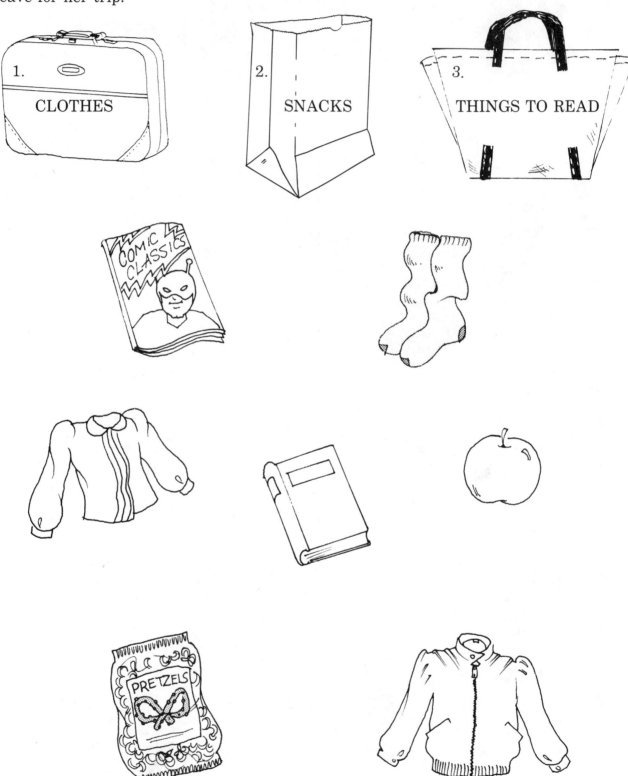

You made it just in time!

Move It!

Help the movers put these things in the right rooms of the house. Draw a line from each picture to the room of the house where it belongs.

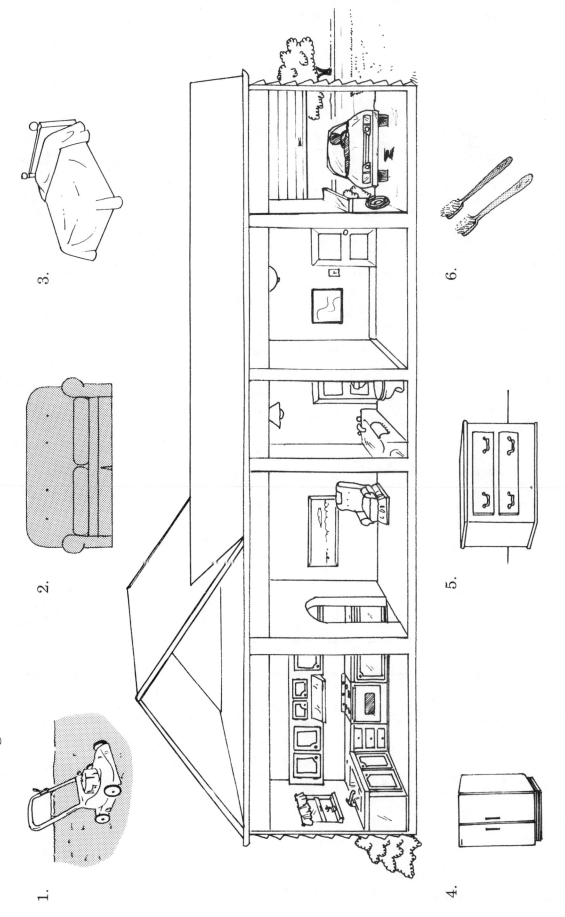

Name _____

1.

2.

3.

4.

5.

6.

You're ready to move in!

ASSOCIATIONS

19

Copyright © 1988 LinguiSystems, Inc.

These Don't Belong!

Name _____

Look at each row of pictures. Mark an X on the picture in each row that doesn't belong. Then, tell why it doesn't belong.

1.

2.

3.

4.

Your answers are right on the mark!

Light or Heavy?

Name _____

Pick up a big dictionary in the library. It's heavy! Now, pick up a piece of paper. It's light! Look at the pictures below. Color all the pictures that are light with your yellow crayon. Then, color all the pictures that are heavy with your blue crayon.

1.

2.

3.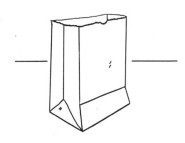

4.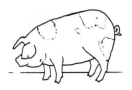

5.

6.

7.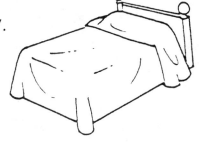

8.

Color this square with your blue crayon. Then, color over the blue with your yellow crayon. What color is the square now?

21

Oceans of Fun

Name _____

Kelly took pictures of her trip to the ocean, but somehow they got mixed up with some other pictures. Circle each picture below that has something to do with the ocean. Then, you'll know what Kelly saw on her trip!

What else could you find at an ocean?

Desert Treasure

Name _____

Look at this old treasure map to find the things that don't belong. Draw a circle around those things when you find them. Then, tell why they don't belong. Finally, draw a line to connect the trail of pictures that are alike until you reach the treasure!

Start here.

1.

2.

3.

4.

5.

6.

Did you reach the desert treasure?

Where on Earth?

Name _____

Fill in this crossword puzzle by reading the clues below. Each set of words gives you clues about where they are found. The first letter of each word is given as an extra clue.

Across

1. slide, swings, seesaw
2. closet, dresser, bed
3. sink, toaster, stove
4. nurse, pills, rooms

Down

2. sand, pail, lifeguard
5. seeds, flower, dirt
6. fish, ship, waves
7. clown, tigers, cotton candy
8. cows, barn, fences

What's your favorite place to be? Why?

Feeling Great!

Some things go together because they feel the same. Look at the pictures below. Draw a line from each picture to the word that describes how the object feels.

1.   2.   3.

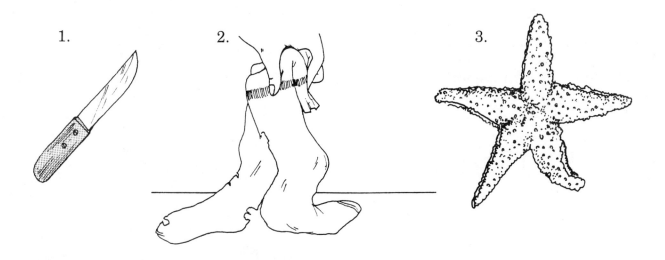

soft   rough   sharp

4.   5.   6.

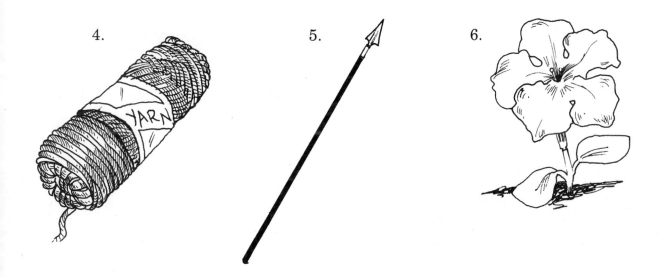

I have a feeling you did very well!

Mixed-up Map

What a crazy map! Find the things that don't belong. Mark them with an X. Then, tell why they don't belong.

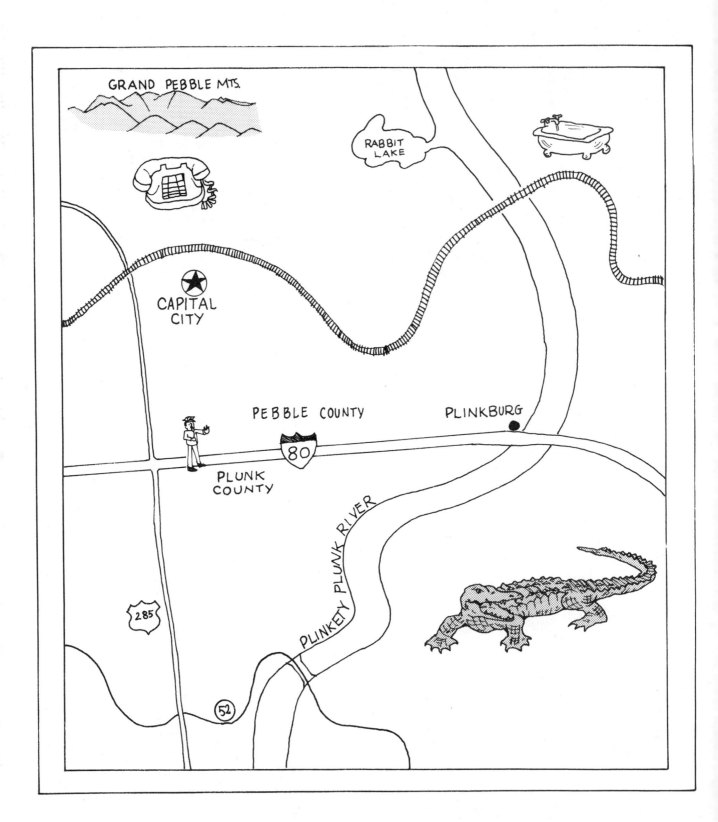

You're a good map reader!

Riddle Ravel

Name _____

Read each riddle below. Then, draw a line from each riddle to the picture that matches its description.

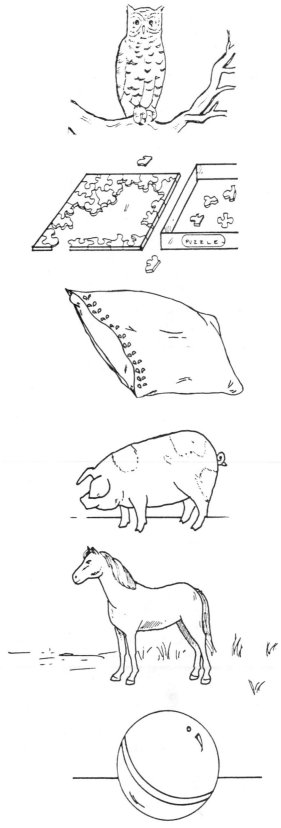

1. I live on a farm.
   I have four legs.
   You can put a saddle on me.
   What am I?

2. I have feathers.
   I can fly.
   I have two legs.
   What am I?

3. I am fun to play with.
   You can share me with friends.
   I bounce.
   What am I?

4. I come in a box.
   I have many pieces.
   You can put me together.
   What am I?

5. I am fat.
   I have a curly tail.
   I like to sit in mud.
   What am I?

6. I am soft.
   I go on a bed.
   You can put your head on me.
   What am I?

Now, make up your own riddle. Tell it to a friend. See if your friend can figure it out.

Leo the Lion

Name _____

Help Leo the Lion match the words below with the right pictures. Write each word on a line under the picture it goes with.

leaves	barking
feathers	trunk
gallop	hooves
paws	puppies
wings	branches
neigh	beak

1.

_____
_____
_____

2.

_____
_____
_____

3.

_____
_____
_____

4.

_____
_____
_____

"Lovely work!" says Leo the Lion.

Around and Around

Name _____

Draw a circle around the category name for each picture below. Be sure to read each category before you choose the correct one.

vehicle

vegetable

toy

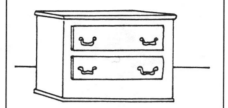

kitchen furniture

livingroom furniture

bedroom furniture

something to write with

something to wear

something to read

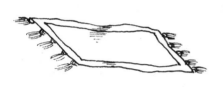

something in the sky

something you trace

something on the floor

wild animal

farm animal

tame animal

vegetable

fruit

dairy product

building

room

office

game

dish

machine

body part

fruit

design

You deserve a round of applause!

All Together Now

Look at the rows of pictures below. Find the one that does not belong in each row and draw a line through it. Why do the others go together? Write your answer on the line below the pictures.

1.

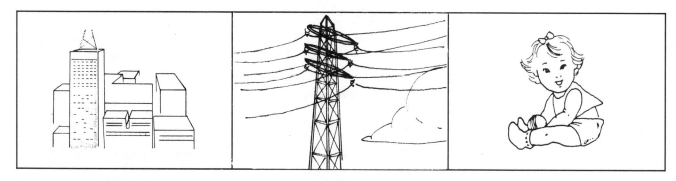

_____

2.

_____

3.

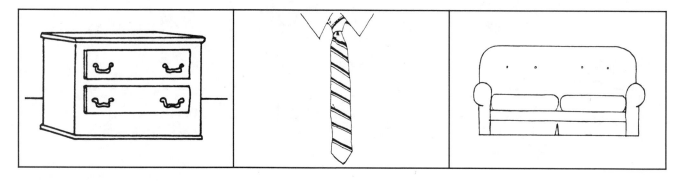

_____

You figured it all out!

Strong Connections

Read the words in the box below. Then, write each word under the correct category. Use all of the words!

book	penny	adult
hospital	grandfather	island
stranger	village	wagon
meadow	wife	uncle
blanket	garden	mirror

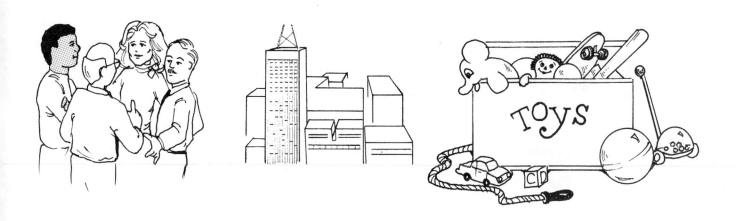

People	Places	Things
_____	_____	_____
_____	_____	_____
_____	_____	_____
_____	_____	_____
_____	_____	_____
_____	_____	_____

What's one word for people, places, and things?

31

Yum, Yum!

Name _____

The foods we eat go together in special ways. Read the list of foods below. Then, write the letter of the correct food group beside each kind of food. Hurry! I'm getting hungry!

FOODS

1. _____ fish

2. _____ butter

3. _____ carrots

4. _____ cheese

5. _____ chicken

6. _____ milk

7. _____ muffin

8. _____ banana

9. _____ biscuit

10. _____ beets

11. _____ bacon

12. _____ ice cream

13. _____ steak

14. _____ oats

FOOD GROUPS

A. Dairy Products

B. Breads and Cereals

C. Meats

D. Fruits and Vegetables

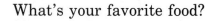

What's your favorite food?

Calling All Categories

Name _____

Fill in this crossword puzzle with the name of the category for each set of clues.

Across

1. sparrow, robin, blue jay
2. breakfast, lunch, supper
3. anger, joy, sadness
4. baseball, soccer, football

Down

1. strawberry, raspberry, blackberry
5. gun, cannon, slingshot
6. Mars, Earth, Saturn
7. thief, robber, bandit
8. oats, wheat, soybeans

You're in a category all by yourself!

Out of Place

Name _____

Read the words in each row. Find the word that doesn't belong with the other three.
Write the letter of your answer in the blank. Then, tell why that word doesn't belong
with the others.

1. _____   A. in   B. on   C. said   D. under

2. _____   A. lunch   B. supper   C. breakfast   D. apple

3. _____   A. table   B. chair   C. bench   D. sofa

4. _____   A. rose   B. ribbon   C. tulip   D. carnation

5. _____   A. newspaper   B. book   C. glove   D. recipe

6. _____   A. guard   B. pitcher   C. shortstop   D. catcher

7. _____   A. short   B. wide   C. tall   D. purple

8. _____   A. freezer   B. sink   C. couch   D. counter

9. _____   A. October   B. Easter   C. August   D. June

10. _____ A. ring   B. bracelet   C. necklace   D. brush

11. _____ A. paper   B. jump rope   C. race car   D. puzzle

12. _____ A. refrigerator B. ice cube   C. diamond   D. igloo

13. _____ A. hammer   B. screwdriver C. toolbox   D. wrench

14. _____ A. smooth   B. happy   C. bumpy   D. rough

15. _____ A. eraser   B. crayon   C. chalk   D. pencil

Your nice work takes first place!

A Colorful Day

Name _____

Let's read a story! Then, we'll answer some questions about the story. Are you ready? Here we go!

"What a beautiful day," thought Renee. The air was warm and the sky was bright blue. Fluffy white clouds looked like cotton. The grass was as green as an emerald. Renee loved spring. On her way to school, she saw a beautiful red cardinal eating seeds with its yellow beak. A little brown rabbit hopped out from behind a bush to watch her. There were pink, red, and yellow tulips in every garden Renee saw. "The thing I like most about spring is the colors," she said.

Look at the underlined words in the story. Why do these words go together? Write your answer on the line below.

_____

Now, color the picture to match the colors in the story.

What's your favorite color? Name five things that are that color.

Planting Time

Name _____

Vincent is getting ready for spring planting. He needs to plant the same kinds of things together. Help him sort out the seeds by writing the letter of the plant category beside each plant. Be careful! They aren't all flowers, vegetables, or trees!

A. Flower   B. Vegetable   C. Tree   D. Other

1. _____ squash

2. _____ maple

3. _____ rose

4. _____ turnip

5. _____ alfalfa

6. _____ beets

7. _____ birch

8. _____ tulip

9. _____ wheat

10. _____ cabbage

11. _____ elm

12. _____ soybeans

13. _____ ash

14. _____ pumpkin

15. _____ daisy

16. _____ spruce

17. _____ pine

18. _____ onion

19. _____ lily

20. _____ oak

What kind of plants are in the Other category? _____

Vincent is bound to have a beautiful garden!

Everything in Common

Name _____

Read each sentence below. Then, tell why the underlined words go together. Write your answers below the sentences.

1. The children honored the <u>custodians</u>, <u>teachers</u>, and <u>secretaries</u> for all their hard work.

   _____

2. A <u>gallon</u> is more than a <u>quart</u>, and a <u>quart</u> is more than a <u>pint</u>.

   _____

3. The United States has two <u>oceans</u>, a <u>gulf</u>, and five large <u>lakes</u> along its borders.

   _____

4. The antique <u>bracelet</u>, <u>necklace</u>, and <u>earrings</u> are worth $1,000.

   _____

5. Stephanie brought <u>sandals</u>, <u>tennis shoes</u>, and <u>boots</u> to camp.

   _____

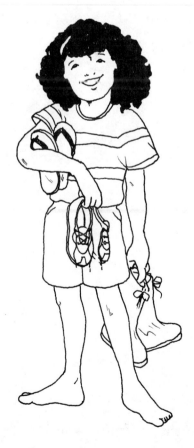

Super answers!

Pioneer Days

Look at the village of Walnut Grove below. Name as many things in the picture as you can, using words from the box. Then, tell why the words that are left in the box don't belong in Walnut Grove.

general store	jail	wagon	skyscraper
log cabin	harnesses	telephone	horses
cars	mill	hitch	radio
saddle	electricity	skateboard	bank

Have you ever seen a town like this? Would you like to live here?

Be a Good Sport

Name _____

How much do you know about sports? In the left column below are different sports terms. In the right column are the names of three different sports. Write the letter of the sport beside the appropriate terms.

1. _____ diamond

2. _____ guard

3. _____ tackle

4. _____ hoop

5. _____ goal line

6. _____ bunt

7. _____ dribble

8. _____ kickoff

9. _____ touchdown

10. _____ pitcher

11. _____ shoot

12. _____ home run

13. _____ field

14. _____ forward

15. _____ free throw

16. _____ pop fly

17. _____ court

18. _____ inning

19. _____ yard line

20. _____ home plate

A. Basketball

B. Football

C. Baseball

You just scored your own victory!

Home at Last

Name _____

Animals live in all sorts of places. In the left column below are the names of some animals. In the right column are some places where animals live. Write the letter of the place where each animal lives beside its name.

1. _____ walrus
2. _____ zebra
3. _____ wolves
4. _____ piglet
5. _____ raccoon
6. _____ whale
7. _____ ape
8. _____ wildcat
9. _____ dolphin
10. _____ polar bear
11. _____ leopard
12. _____ collie
13. _____ seal
14. _____ rhinoceros
15. _____ penguin
16. _____ trout
17. _____ woodchuck
18. _____ chick
19. _____ chimpanzee
20. _____ colt

A. Jungle

B. Farm

C. Water

D. Forest

E. Arctic

What kind of animals do you like best?

Make a Choice!

Name _____

Underline the correct word in the parentheses to finish each sentence. Read carefully!

1. Bronze, copper, and silver are (awards, metals).

2. Cannons, torpedoes, and missiles are military (weapons, buildings).

3. Bitter, sweet, and sour are different (smells, tastes).

4. Drapes, curtains, and shades are (window, door) coverings.

5. Gas, oil, and wood are (fuels, engines).

6. Lumber, cement, and bricks are (cleaning, building) materials.

7. Mosquitoes, moths, and ladybugs are (reptiles, insects).

8. Postcards, magazines, and letters are types of (mail, books).

"Choice" answers, indeed!

41

Solid or Liquid?

Name _____

Some things go together because they're solids or liquids. Look in your science book or dictionary to find out what solids and liquids are. Write the definitions of these words on the lines below. Then, write S by the words that are solids and L by the words that are liquids.

Solid _____

_____

Liquid _____

_____

1. armchair _____   13. blueberry _____

2. battery _____   14. blood _____

3. juice _____   15. dome _____

4. belt _____   16. windshield _____

5. moth _____   17. gasoline _____

6. broth _____   18. icicle _____

7. raindrop _____   19. fabric _____

8. ladle _____   20. water _____

9. boulder _____   21. window _____

10. pier _____   22. husk _____

11. canoe _____   23. coffee _____

12. rain _____   24. vinegar _____

Your work is solid as a rock!

Everything's Coming Up Roses!

Name _____

The roses in this garden need a little color! Read the words in the roses and color them according to the color code in the box. I'm sure you'll have beautiful results!

CATEGORY	CODE
instrument	pink
vegetable	red
toy or game	yellow
emotion	orange

1. anger
2. doll
3. onion
4. flute
5. peas
6. skates
7. piano
8. joy
9. baseball
10. trombone
11. pride
12. lettuce
13. football
14. greed
15. violin
16. corn

You do "rosey" work!

Fill It In

Look at the word in the center of each box below. On each line around the box,
write a word that goes with the word in the center. The first one is done for you.

1. _____detective_____

_____custodian_____   _____magician_____

| CAREER |

_____editor_____   _____pilot_____

_____scientist_____

2. _____

_____   _____

| HOBBY |

_____   _____

_____

3. _____

_____   _____

| DISEASE |

_____   _____

_____

4. _____

_____   _____

| RELATIVE |

_____   _____

_____

5. _____

_____   _____

| HOLIDAY |

_____   _____

_____

Did you fill in all the blanks? Good!

It's Your Choice

Name _____

Read the words in the boxes below. Then, underline the word to the right of each box that tells why the words go together.

1.

spine abdomen fingernail calf liver

clean things
parts of an arm
plants
body parts

2.

attorney chemist veterinarian zookeeper janitor

occupations
foreigners
buildings
students

3.

baboon caribou falcon mink muskrat

baby animals
pets
wild animals
animals we ride

4.

bathrobe parka blouse earmuffs muffler

cartoons
clothes
things we fold
jewelry

Now, think of three more words that go with each category. Write the words in the blanks below.

1. _____

_____

_____

2. _____

_____

_____

3. _____

_____

_____

4. _____

_____

_____

What are three words you could use to describe your work on this page?

Vocabulary Quiz

Name _____

Underline the words in each row that are like the boxed word. Circle the word that doesn't belong with the others. Then, write the reason it doesn't belong.

1. | hospital | physician   medicine   recreation   surgeon

_____

_____

2. | adore | love   honor   cherish   despise

_____

_____

3. | chat | gossip   stare   converse   discuss

_____

_____

4. | downpour | drizzle   icicle   raindrop   shower

_____

_____

5. | decade | second   century   year   months

_____

_____

Your vocabulary IQ is very high!

Closely Linked

Name _____

Look at the groups of words below. Circle the word in each group that doesn't belong.
Then, write the reason all the other words go together.

1.

streetcar

battleship

banister

submarine

motorcycle

_____

_____

_____

2.

comrade

mechanic

janitor

surgeon

attorney

_____

_____

_____

3.

amber

dark

turquoise

periwinkle

crimson

_____

_____

_____

4.

apricot

tangerine

kiwi

potato

strawberry

_____

_____

_____

Now, name another word that fits into each group above.

Synonyms

Children learn the features of words and their synonyms rather matter-of-factly, almost casually, as they grow and interact with their environment. To be able to identify a synonym for a specific word, a child must know the critical semantic attributes of the target word so she can retrieve a semantically-like word from her vocabulary.

The language-delayed child may have difficulty with the synonym task because she focuses on the incorrect feature of a word when naming its synonym. For example, a child who says "building" is a synonym for "home" is not focusing on the residential feature of the word "home," and the answer "building" is not specific enough. Language-delayed children must be shown that the semantic features of the target word and its synonym are almost identical.

Some language-delayed children may be too specific when trying to complete the synonym task. For example, a child who says the synonym for "emotion" is "angry" recognizes only that "angry" is a specific type of emotion. This response indicates that the child does not understand the need for a word that fulfills the general synonym requirements, such as the word "feeling."

Language-delayed children also must learn that gradations in the meaning of synonyms add flavor and color to our language. A child might only know "large" as the synonym for "big." Imagine how much more accurately she could describe her environment if she also knew the words "huge, gigantic, hefty, spacious," and "extensive," and could use them in the appropriate contexts!

Being able to express a one-word synonym is a task required in every classroom. These Synonyms worksheets help children to recognize critical semantic attributes of words in order to identify synonyms.

Listen to these sentences. Say each sentence after me, but change the last word. Make sure your new sentence means the same thing I said.

1. The rabbit jumped into the bag.

2. Andrew picked up a small rock.

Now, change some other words in the sentences, without changing what the sentences mean. Then, color the pictures for your good work!

Change Up!

Listen to these sentences. Say each sentence after me, but change one of the underlined words. Make sure your new sentence means the same thing I said.

1. The <u>children</u> <u>watched</u> the <u>beautiful</u> <u>woman</u>.

2. <u>Dad</u> <u>cleans</u> the <u>car</u> <u>every</u> Saturday.

Now, change some other words in the sentences, without changing what the sentences mean. Job well done!

Say These Two Ways!

Name _____

Listen to these sentences. Say each sentence after me, but change two of the underlined words in the sentence. Then, we'll write down your new sentence. Make sure your sentence means the same thing I said.

1. The <u>happy</u> <u>cook</u> <u>fixed</u> some lemonade.

2. The <u>small</u> <u>boy</u> on the <u>boat</u> is wearing a <u>jacket</u> and a <u>cap</u>.

Circle the words you changed in your sentences. Nice changes!

52

Name _____

Tell Me Again!

Look at the picture below. There are a lot of things happening. Tell me what you see.

Now, tell me about the picture again. This time, use different words for all the shaded parts of the picture.

In Your Own Words

Name _____

Let's read a story. First, I'll read it. Then, we can read it together. When we read the story together, you can name the pictures. Use different words than I used the first time, but make sure the words mean the same thing.

Going Shopping

Andrea and Josh needed some new clothes. Andrea wanted a new 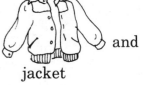 and
jacket

Josh needed a new to wear for baseball. Their took them
cap   mother

to the clothing . Both found the clothes they wanted, and
store   children

they were very happy. Josh wore his , but Andrea carried her
cap

 in a . They were so happy, their mom decided to have their

jacket   sack

 taken. Andrea and Josh both looked at the camera with big  !

photo   grins

You tell a good story!

Think of a Different Way

Name _____

Listen to these sentences. Then, change as many words as you can, but make sure each sentence means the same thing.

1. The police looked for the thief in the forest.

2. Grandpa pounded nails in the cellar.

Good thinking!

How Sharp Are You?

Name _____

Look closely at the picture below. There are at least five things in the picture that have two names. Color each of these things. Then, write their names in the blanks.

1. _____   _____

2. _____   _____

3. _____   _____

4. _____   _____

5. _____   _____

Are you "shore" you've found all of them?

Help Tell a Story!

Let's read a story. First, I'll read it. Then, we can read it together. When we read the story together, you can name the pictures. Use different words than I used the first time, but make sure the words mean the same thing.

Job Time

One afternoon, Adrian came home from basketball practice. His mother had left this message on the refrigerator:

"I went to work. I'll be back at 5:00. There's a cup of milk and a fruit salad for you in the fridge. Please take the dishes out of the dishwasher and put them away. Then, empty the wastebasket into a garbage bag and put it beside the street . Thanks! Love, Mom"

You're a good storyteller!

Face Up to It!

Name _____

Show how you feel when you're mad, glad, or sad. Draw a face on each head to show these feelings. Then, think of another word to describe each face. Write the new words in the blanks.

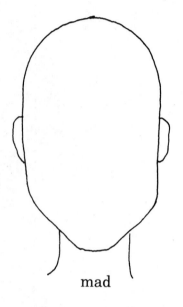
mad

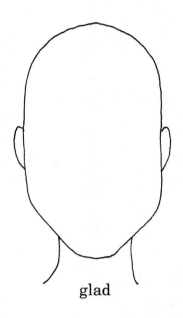
glad

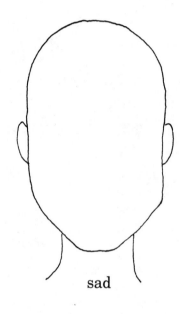
sad

1. _____   2. _____   3. _____

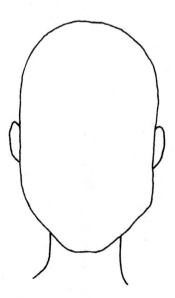

Draw how you feel today.

Twice as Nice

Name _____

Use two different words to describe each picture. Think and think again!

1. _____

   _____

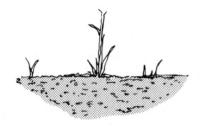

2. _____

   _____

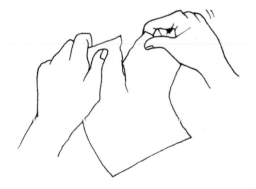

3. _____

   _____

4. _____

   _____

Good! Now, tell me a word that means the same as *forest*. Then, draw a picture of it on the back of your worksheet.

Double Duty

Name _____

Draw a line from each word to the picture it matches. Then, think of another word that means the same thing. Write that word beside the picture.

1. plates

_____

2. sick

_____

3. shore

_____

4. path

_____

What's another word for instructor? Draw a picture of your new word on the back of your worksheet.

60

Are You on the Ball?

Name _____

Tell where the ball is in each picture. We'll write your answer on the first line. Then, think of another way to say the same thing. We'll write your second answer on the bottom line.

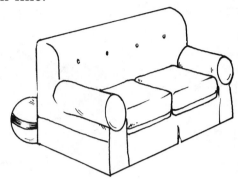

1. _____

_____

2. _____

_____

3. _____

_____

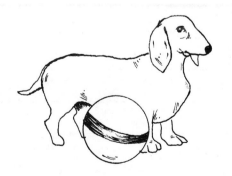

4. _____

_____

Now, put your pencil below this paper. Think of another word that tells where your pencil is.

Double Trouble

Name _____

The car has broken down and no one is around! Help the driver think of two words for each part of the picture that has an arrow pointing to it. Write the words in the blanks.

1. _____   _____

2. _____   _____

3. _____   _____

4. _____   _____

5. _____   _____

What season is it? Can you think of two words for that season? You're a good word mechanic!

Missing Vowels

Name _____

These crossword puzzles are missing the vowels. Put in the correct vowels and you'll discover two words that mean the same thing.

Vowels: a e i o u

1.
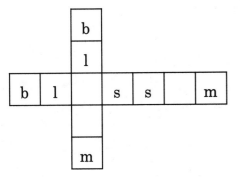

2.

3.
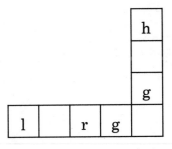

4.
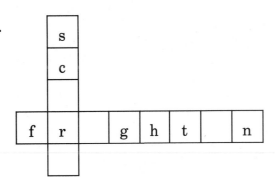

5.
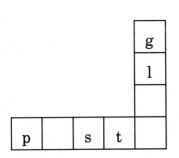

6.
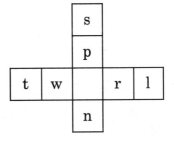

7.

Now, you are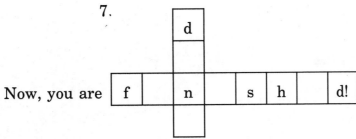

Name It Again

Can you think of two names for each picture? Sure! Of course! Look at the first letter of each word to get started. The first one is done for you.

1. c h a m p i o n

    w i n n e r

2. t __ __ __ __ __ __ __

    c __ __ __ __ __ __

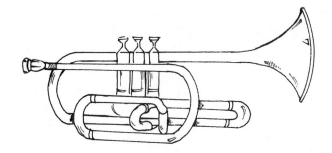

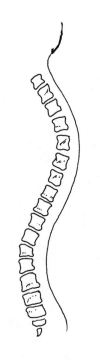

3. s __ __ __ __

    b __ __ __ __ __ __

4. c __ __ __ __ __

    s __ __ __ __ __ __

If this was simple for you, it must have been e ___ ___ ___ !

Describe This!   Name _____

Look at the picture below. Then, fill in the blanks to describe the picture.

1. A _____ and a _____ are on the _____

2. There are _____ on the chair.

Now, write each sentence again and change each word that's in a blank. Make sure each sentence means the same thing. Good luck!

1. _____

2. _____

Make Your Choice

Name _____

Choose a synonym from the box to complete each sentence.

demand	timid	trash
hare	author	silent

1. If you are shy, then you are _____ .

2. One kind of rabbit is called a _____ .

3. When you are _____ , you are quiet.

4. A writer can also be called an _____ .

5. When you insist on something, you _____ that it be done.

6. When you take out the garbage, you're also taking out the _____ .

Your selections were choice!

Puzzling Word Puzzles

Name _____

Now's your time to *shine*! Do your *sparkling* best to solve these word puzzles. Fill in the letters in each puzzle so the two words are synonyms. You can do it!

1.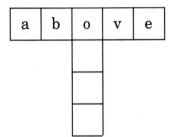

2.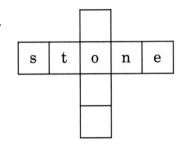

3.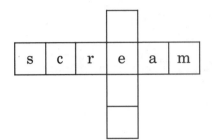

4.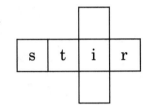

5.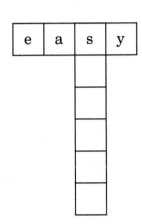

6.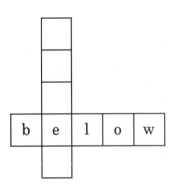

7.

8.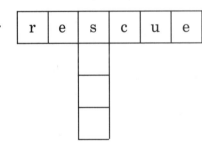

9.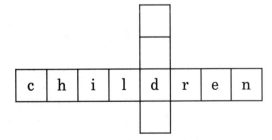

Positively puzzling!

Match 'em Up

Draw lines to match the words in the right column with the descriptions in the left column.

1. When you smile a little, you _____ .   mistake

2. If someone makes an error, she makes a _____ .   joyful

3. When I'm fearful, I'm _____ .   lid

4. If you're cheerful, you're also _____ .   grin

5. The top of a box is also its _____ .   frightened

6. When fruit is rotten, it has _____ .   wound

7. Someone with an injury has a _____ .   strange

8. A dress that is unusual looks _____ .   spoiled

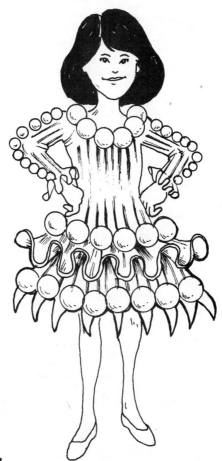

You're a great match-maker!

Triple Trouble

After each sentence below are three words. Choose the word that is a synonym for the underlined word in the sentence. Then, cross out the underlined word and write the synonym above it.

1. Janelle likes to get up at <u>daybreak</u>.   dusk, dawn, noon

2. Martinez was <u>confused</u> by the directions, so he asked his teacher for help.   annoyed, terrified, bewildered

3. The nursery <u>selected</u> flowers that would grow well in the shade.   chose, connected, detested

4. After the show, we saw the <u>advertisement</u> for Disney World.   monument, entertainment, commercial

5. The <u>dolphin</u> was trained to leap out of the water.   diver, porpoise, gulf

You did very well!

Double Letters

Can you think of the synonyms for these words? Each synonym has a set of double letters. Fill in the other letters for each word.

1. stream   __ __ e e __

2. ordinary   __ __ m m __ __

3. autumn   __ __ l l

4. chest   __ __ __ s s __ __

5. hard   __ __ f f __ __ __ __ __

6. awful   __ __ r r __ __ __ __

7. sick   __ l l

8. crash   __ c c __ __ __ __

9. university   __ __ l l __ __ __

10. laugh   __ __ g g __ __

llama

__ oo __ job!

Same Starts

Name _____

Each of these synonym pairs starts with the same letter. Fill in the rest of each puzzle with the synonym for the word already given.

1.
s					
t
e
p
s

2.
b					
e
l
o
w

3.
a		
s
s
i
s
t

4.
s			
y
m
b
o
l

5.
l			
e
n
g
t
h
y

6.
j				
a
m

7.
j					
u
b
i
l
a
n
t

Good detective work!

Take Your Choice!

Name _____

Fill in the blank in each sentence with a synonym for the word below the blank.
Choose synonyms from the box.

damp	statue	forecasted
entertainment	motioned	witness

1. The circus is always excellent _____ .

amusement

2. My friend _____ for me to stop by his desk.

gestured

3. The picnic table was _____ from the dew.

moist

4. Our city built a _____ of Martin Luther King.

monument

5. The police officer questioned the _____ .

observer

6. The weather expert _____ a 70% chance of snow.

predicted

You made some fine choices!

Cross Synonym Puzzle

Name _____

Here's a crossword puzzle made up of synonyms. The beginning of each word and a clue are given for you. G ___ ___ ___ luck!

Across

1. wedding
2. teach
3. TV advertisement
4. attorney
5. something that is very old
6. person who flies a plane
7. a school people attend after high school

Down

3. to be in charge of
8. something that doesn't happen very often
9. needed
10. the space in a house just below the roof
11. humor

Use the dictionary if you need to!

A Bunch of Synonyms

Fill in the blanks in each sentence with a synonym for the word below the blank. Choose synonyms from the box. Every synonym begins with the letter *a*! Ready, set, *attack*!

average	amount	awkward	aisle
annoys	advice	apprentice	ability

1. My little brother always _____ me when I'm studying.

bothers

2. Ted looked at the cash register and couldn't believe the _____ he had to pay.

total

3. Although her mother is very tall, Sheila is of _____ height.

medium

4. The new _____ has a lot of natural _____ .

trainee   talent

5. The usher was very _____ as he came down the _____ .

clumsy   walkway

6. The teacher asked the principal for some _____ .

suggestions

You deserve an A+!

True or False?

Name _____

Here are some true and false statements. Answer each one by circling T for a true statement and F for a false statement. Then, think of how you can make each false sentence true by changing one word. Write down your new sentence below the old one. Good luck!

T   F   1. A tourist is a traveler.

_____

T   F   2. If you look at a compass, you can tell what the temperature is.

_____

T   F   3. A coward is someone who is very brave.

_____

T   F   4. Sunset is the same time as dusk.

_____

T   F   5. A violet dress is a shade of crimson.

_____

T   F   6. A team that is victorious is triumphant.

_____

T   F   7. If a doctor prescribes pills for you, you might take tablets.

_____

T   F   8. An orchard of orange trees can also be called a timber.

_____

You're a true worker!

Find the Synonyms

Here are four pictures with a sentence to describe each one. Write each sentence using synonyms for at least two of the underlined words.

1. The <u>hairless</u> <u>father</u> is holding the <u>crying</u> <u>baby</u>.

_____

_____

2. The coach was <u>ecstatic</u> <u>because</u> his <u>players</u> won the game.

_____

_____

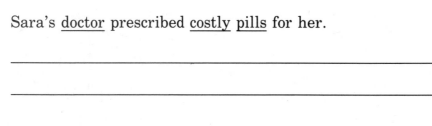

3. <u>Everyone</u> <u>admired</u> the heroine for her <u>brave</u> <u>actions</u>.

_____

_____

4. Sara's <u>doctor</u> prescribed <u>costly</u> <u>pills</u> for her.

_____

_____

Super sentences!

You Be the Writer!

Name _____

Now, it's your turn to create. Write a sentence to describe each picture below. Then, write the same sentence again, using a synonym for at least one of the words from your first sentence.

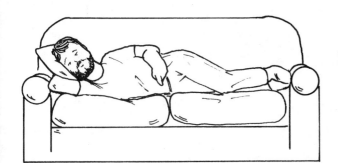

1. _____

_____

_____

_____

2. _____

_____

_____

_____

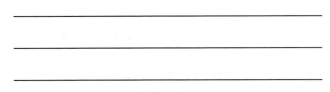

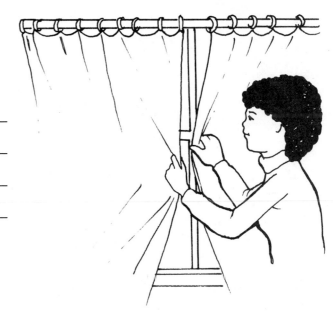

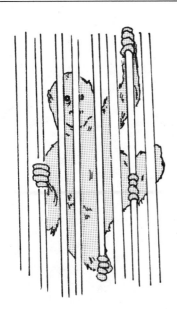

3. _____

_____

_____

_____

You're quite an author!

It's in the Bag

Name _____

Choose synonyms from the bag to complete each of the sentences. You can do it!

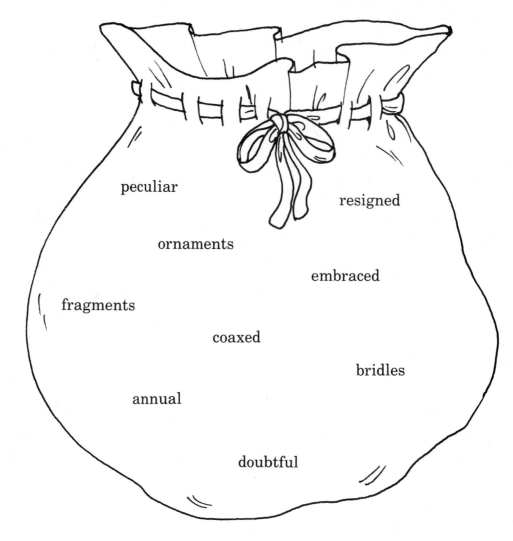

peculiar

resigned

ornaments

embraced

fragments

coaxed

bridles

annual

doubtful

1. My mom always has her _____ physical examination in January.
   yearly

2. The manager _____ her job to go back to school.
   quit

3. Brad _____ his brother to enter the race.
   urged

4. Daffodils have a very _____ scent.
   odd

5. On Christmas, we put all the _____ on our tree.
   decorations

6. The police officer picked up _____ of the car after the accident.
   pieces

Way to go!

If You Are...

Name _____

Answer these questions by circling Yes or No. If you answer No, write a synonym for the underlined word in the blank at the end of the line.

Yes   No   1. If you are <u>dependable</u>, are you reliable? _____

Yes   No   2. If you are <u>snickering</u>, are you complaining? _____

Yes   No   3. If you are <u>researching</u> something, are you investigating? _____

Yes   No   4. If you <u>hurt</u> yourself, do you inquire yourself? _____

Yes   No   5. If you <u>taunt</u> someone, are you teasing? _____

Yes   No   6. If you are <u>humorous</u>, are you fragile? _____

Did you get them all right? If you did, everything was correct!

Three-Way Tricky Crosswords

Name _____

Each of the words in a crossword mean the same thing. One of the words is spelled out for you and the first letters of the other crosswords are provided. Have fun filling in the missing letters!

1.

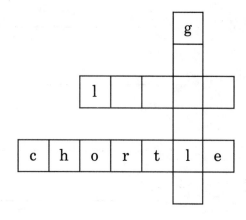

2.

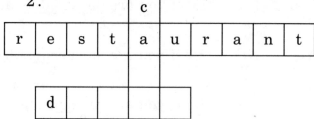

2.

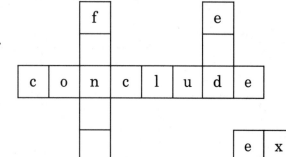

4.

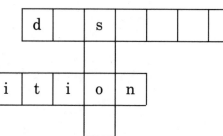

5.

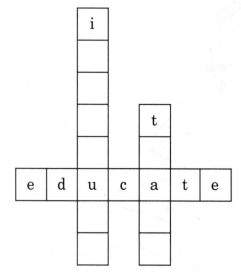

6.

Very nice!

Answer Two Ways!

Name _____

Look at the pictures and questions below. Write your answer to the question on the first line. Then, write your answer again, using a synonym for the word you wrote first.

What is the woman doing?

1. _____ a pair of pants

   _____ a pair of pants

Where do we put clean dishes?

2. in the _____

   in the _____

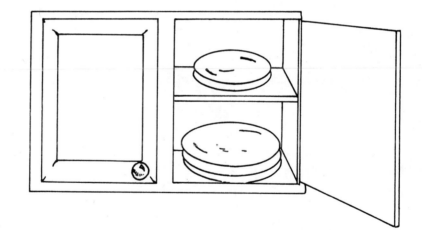

Where can you find tombstones?

3. in a _____

   in a _____

You're doing fine! You're doing well!

81

Three's a Charm

Name _____

After each sentence below are three words. Choose the one that is a synonym for the underlined word. Then, cross out the underlined word and write the synonym above it.

1. The <u>tragedy</u> brought the entire town together.

filth, disaster, fugitive

2. Ike and Fernando like to <u>trade</u> baseball cards.

swap, smack, shrivel

3. Many fish <u>died</u> because of the oil slick.

consented, grieved, perished

4. The salesperson <u>convinced</u> Dad to buy the more expensive lawn mower.

persuaded, soothed, pursued

5. I handled the <u>breakable</u> vase very carefully.

flexible, antique, fragile

6. Our coach sent in a <u>replacement</u> for the pitcher.

substitute, scholar, specimen

Way to go!

Double Clues

Can you think of the synonyms for these words? Each synonym has a set of double letters. Fill in the other letters for each word.

1. absent   ____ ____ s s ____ ____ ____

2. flag   ____ ____ n n ____ ____

3. corridor   ____ ____ l l ____ ____ ____

4. mistake   ____ r r ____ ____

5. huge   ____ m m ____ ____ ____ ____

6. defeat   ____ ____ s s

7. job   ____ c c ____ ____ ____ ____ ____ ____ ____

8. rumor   ____ ____ s s ____ ____

9. harden   ____ ____ ____ f f ____ ____

10. own   ____ ____ s s ____ s s

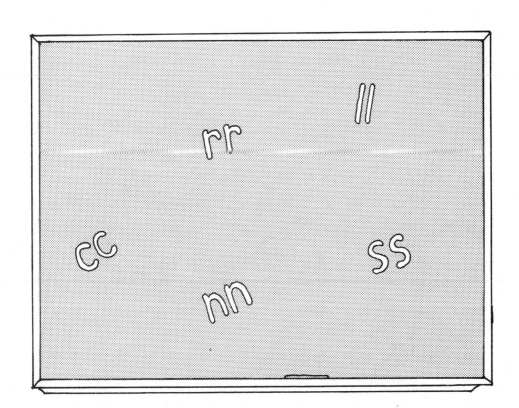

You are ____ oo much!

Can You Match These?

Name _____

Finish each sentence with a word from the right column. Be careful! You won't use all the words in the column.

1. A brave person is _____ .

2. When something turns, it _____ .

3. Workers can also be called _____ .

4. The occupant of a house is its _____ .

5. The jewel thief was a sly _____ .

6. A deadly disease can also be called _____ .

7. The airborne jet is still _____ .

8. When our dog fetches a stick, he _____ it quickly.

burglar

courageous

aloft

retrieves

fatal

dismissal

employees

rotates

inhabitant

hesitant

Which sentence does the picture go with? Write your answer here. _____

Which of Three?

After each sentence below are three words. Choose the one that's a synonym for the underlined word. Then, cross out the underlined word and write the synonym above it.

1. Marilyn waited as the <u>walker</u> passed in front of her car.

   treason, pedestrian, spectator

2. Before his speech, Jerome started to <u>sweat</u>.

   perspire, vibrate, tinker

3. The house next to ours is <u>vacant</u>.

   worthless, empty, immense

4. The doctor performed the <u>operation</u> in less than two hours.

   proportion, investigation, surgery

5. Jennifer's job is to purchase <u>clothing</u> for the department store.

   doormats, pigments, garments

6. The skiers barely escaped the <u>snowslide</u>.

   avalanche, souvenir, obstacle

You deserve three ribbons!

Crossword Stumpers

Name _____

All the words in each crossword below mean the same thing. One of the words is spelled out for you and the first letters of the other crosswords are provided. Fill in the missing letters. Do your best!

1.
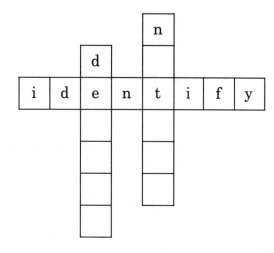

2.
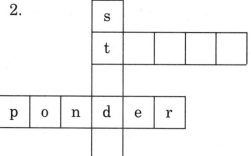

3.
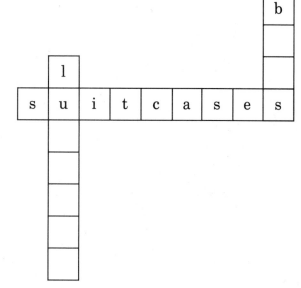

4.

5.

6.

WOW!

Your Turn to Write

Name _____

In the book below are fifteen words. Find the five pairs of synonyms, and write the words in the short blanks. Then, write a sentence for each of the ten words. (Hint: You won't use all of the words.)

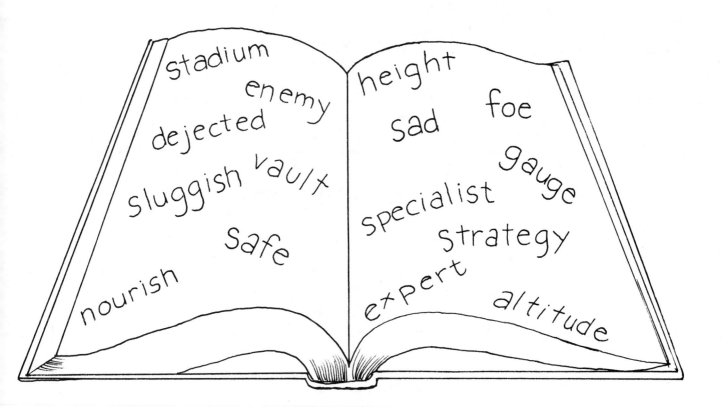

1. _____ _____

   _____

2. _____ _____

   _____

3. _____ _____

   _____

4. _____ _____

   _____

5. _____ _____

   _____

You may be a writer someday!

To Tell the Truth   Name _____

Here are some true and false statements. Answer each one by circling T for a true statement and F for a false statement. Then, think how you can make each false sentence true by changing one word. Write down your new sentence below the old one. Be truthful!

T   F   1. If you are given a boost, you've received a lift.

_____

T   F   2. When you're drowsy, you're alert.

_____

T   F   3. Something that is probable is likely to happen.

_____

T   F   4. A trench is like a ditch.

_____

T   F   5. If you're a specialist, you're an apprentice.

_____

T   F   6. A lawyer presents evidence to a navigator.

_____

T   F   7. If your thirst is quenched, you're satisfied.

_____

T   F   8. If you're glum, you feel elated.

_____

To be honest, you did very well!

Be Creative!

Name _____

The crossword puzzle below is already done, but it needs the clues. Write a synonym for each word in the crossword for each clue.

```
                                                        6
                                                        b
      7                   8            1
      r                   i            b   a   r   r   i   e   r
      e                   l                        r
    2                                                i
      a   c   c   o   m   p   l   i   s   h   m   e   n   t
      o                   u                        k
      m                   s        9
      m                   t        t
    3       10                   4
      a   c   q   u   i   r   e      r   e   m   e   d   y
          n               a        f
          l               t        t
          a               e
          w
          f
          u
    5
      e   l   e   v   a   t   e
```

Across   Down

1. _____   6. _____

2. _____   7. _____

3. _____   8. _____

4. _____   9. _____

5. _____   10. _____

Great synonyms!

Semantic Absurdities

In order to recognize that a sentence does not make sense and provide an explanation or correction, children need a great deal of language sophistication. The first critical step in understanding semantic absurdities is knowing the semantic features of key words in a sentence. The second step requires understanding the meaning of most of the other words in the sentence, such as modifiers and prepositions. Next, based on knowledge of the meaning of the individual words, the child must put words together to determine the overall meaning of the sentence. Then, the child must reason about and identify what makes the sentence absurd. This final step involves understanding that an impossible relationship exists between key words in the sentence.

For example, in the sentence "I rang the numbers of the house," a child first understands the meaning of the key words "rang" and "number." Then, he realizes the phrase "of the house" helps determine the overall meaning that the house address is the focus of the sentence. Finally, the child expresses what is absurd and supplies the word that makes the sentence correct. He reasons that numbers can't be *heard*, that they are seen, and names the most common item of a house that *can* be rung — a doorbell.

Language-delayed children have difficulty understanding humor and the many types of figurative language so common to our language. Some language-delayed children do not understand vocabulary of humorous or absurd sentences, while others are unable to verbally reason about sentence context.

Solving semantic absurdities increases a child's flexibility in the use of words and is an important stepping stone in understanding humor and figurative language. These Semantic Absurdities worksheets teach children to recognize and correct language absurdities in sentences. Children's knowledge and processing time will improve as they begin to understand the steps involved in recognizing and correcting semantic absurdities.

Right or Wrong?

Name _____

Look at the pairs of pictures below. One picture in each pair is right and one is wrong.
Circle the pictures that are right. Put an X on the pictures that are wrong. Then, tell
why the pictures are right or wrong.

1.

2.

3.

Did you get everything right?

Hear Ye, Hear Ye!

Derrick has very good hearing. He says he can hear everything that's on the shelf in his room. Do you think he can hear everything? Well, of course not! Look at the things on the shelf and color the things Derrick can't hear.

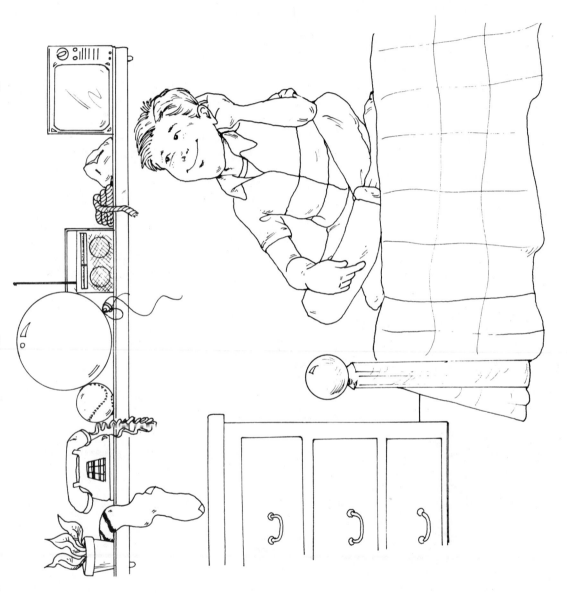

Now, tell why you colored the things you did.

93

A Heavy Load

Look at the pictures at the bottom of the page. Randall put each of these objects in a box marked *HEAVY*. He didn't look at the objects very carefully, did he? Cut each picture out. Put the heavy ones on the left side of the scale, and the other ones on the right side.

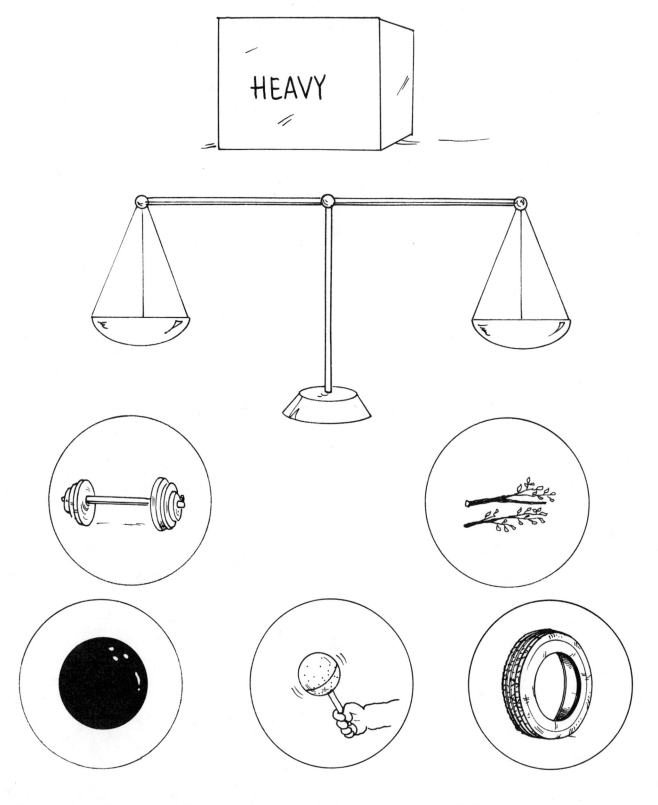

Why was it silly to put all the objects in a box marked *HEAVY*?

Good Night, Nelson!

Nelson likes to stay up late and do things at night. He does some very strange things!
Look at the pictures below and tell which things are silly to do at night.   Then, color
those pictures blue.

1.

2.

3.

4.

5.

6.

Maybe one of these days Nelson will get his days and nights figured out!

Turkey Time

Name _____

Something went wrong at this Thanksgiving dinner! Draw a box around each thing that's wrong in this picture. Then, tell why it's wrong.

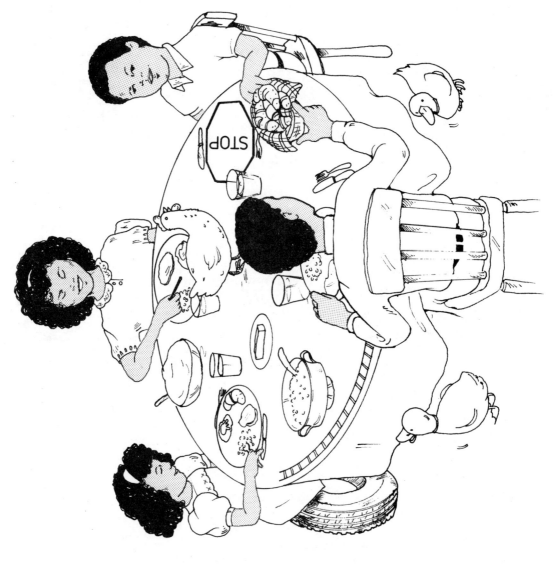

Thank goodness you found everything that was wrong!

Zoo Mix-up

Name _____

Something is terribly wrong at the zoo! The zookeeper needs your help to get things straightened out before the zoo opens. Color the part of each picture that doesn't make sense. Then, tell why it doesn't make sense.

1.

2.

3.

4.

5.

6.

Thanks! Now the zoo can open on time!

A Photo Finish

Name _____

There was a strange race at the county fair last week. Anyone or anything could be in the race! Before the race, the racers were arguing about who was the fastest. Look at each racer below and tell which ones couldn't have won. Then, tell why they couldn't have won. Color the possible winners red! Ready, set, go!

1.

2.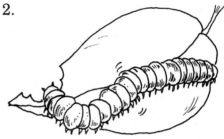

3.

4.

5.

6.

You're the true winner of this race!

Family Trade-off

Name _____

What a hectic morning! Everyone in the Carson family left home with someone else's things. Look at each person. Tell how you know the thing each one took doesn't belong to him. Then, color the thing each person took by mistake.

1.

2.

3.

4.

5.

6.

Nice work! The Carsons will do better tomorrow because of your help!

Picture Perfect!

Name _____

Read the sentences below. Then, circle a word in each sentence that doesn't make sense. Write a new word above each circled word so the sentences make sense. Then, draw pictures of your new sentences in the boxes beside the sentences.

1. I put a straw in my sandwich.

2. I wore my pajamas to the beach.

3. I sleep on a stage.

4. I'm learning how to play the flour.

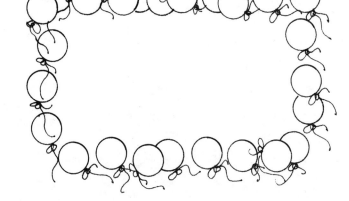

That's much better!

Make It Right!

Name _____

Read the sentences below. The underlined words make the sentences silly. Draw a
line from each underlined word to a picture to take its place. Then, read your new
sentences!

1. I wrote the numbers on my <u>face</u>.

2. I brush my <u>arm</u>.

3. I put a straw in my <u>bed</u>.

4. I drew a <u>circle</u> with straight lines.

5. I float on the <u>sand</u>.

Right on!

Design Your Own

Name _____

Read the sentences below. Then, draw a box around a word in each sentence that doesn't make sense. Write a new word above each boxed word so the sentences make sense. Then, draw pictures of your new sentences in the shapes beside the sentences.

1. I like to swing on elevators.

2. The barge floated in the bathtub.

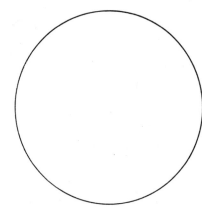

3. I wear my warmest clothes in the summer.

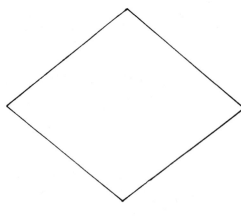

4. I opened the log to get into the yard.

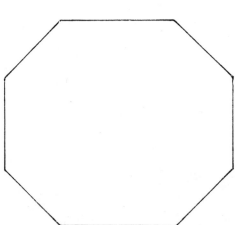

Nice sentences and nice art!

Apple of My Eye

Cut this apple out. Then, cut on the dotted lines to divide the apple into eight pieces.
Next, read the sentences on the apple pieces. Change each sentence so it makes
sense. Finally, paste each piece onto a piece of construction paper to put your apple
back together!

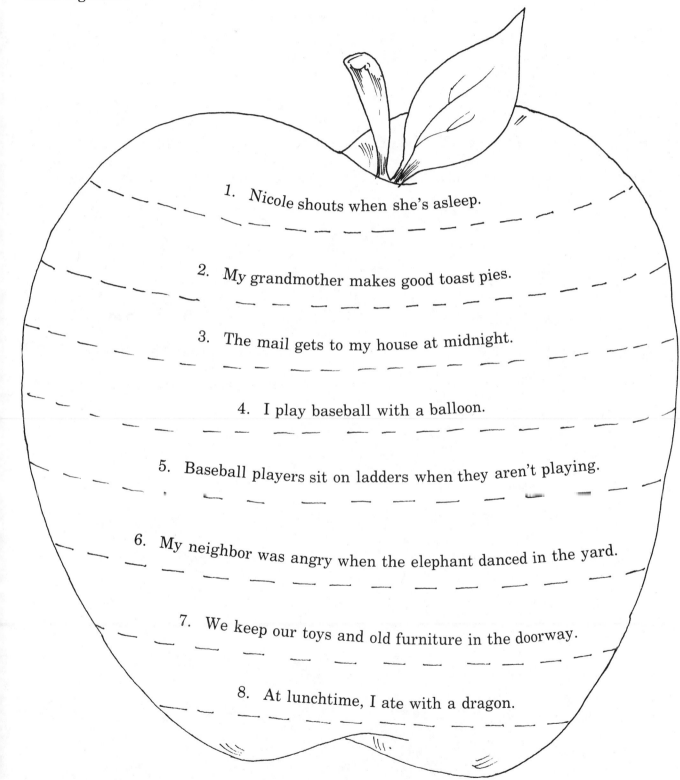

1. Nicole shouts when she's asleep.

2. My grandmother makes good toast pies.

3. The mail gets to my house at midnight.

4. I play baseball with a balloon.

5. Baseball players sit on ladders when they aren't playing.

6. My neighbor was angry when the elephant danced in the yard.

7. We keep our toys and old furniture in the doorway.

8. At lunchtime, I ate with a dragon.

Your apple looks delicious!

103

A Walk to the Park

Name _____

Read the story below. Write words from the box above the underlined words so the story makes sense. Then, read the story again with the right words. It will sound much better with your help!

through	following	store	kitten
young	sunny	noise	outside

One <u>careful</u> day, Allison decided to walk to the park. It was a beautiful day to be <u>overhead</u>! So, she began walking toward the park. Along the way, she saw a <u>late</u> boy who was crying. "What's wrong?" Allison asked the boy. "I can't find my mom," he answered. Well, let's look in this <u>forest</u>. When Allison opened the door, the boy jumped up excitedly. "There's my mom!" he said. "Thank you for helping me find her." "You're welcome," answered Allison. "I'm glad I could help. Good-bye." Allison continued her walk toward the park. She was almost to the park when she heard a <u>bunch</u>. It sounded like a <u>cricket</u> meowing. She looked behind her and there was a kitten <u>choosing</u> her! Allison picked up the kitten. What a friendly meow he had! She decided to call him Tiger because of his orange and black stripes. She held him closely as she slowly walked <u>during</u> the park. "I'm so happy I decided to come to the park today. If I had stayed home, I wouldn't have helped that boy find his mother and I wouldn't have found you, Tiger. I think I'll come to the park more often!"

You did a fine job of straightening out this story!

Appliance Barn

The Appliance Barn is having a big sale. Look at the appliances below to see if you can figure out why they're on sale. Tell what's wrong with each appliance. Then, mark an X on the things that are wrong with the appliances.

1.

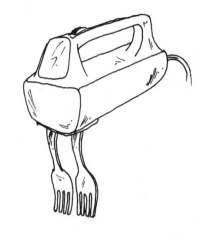

2.

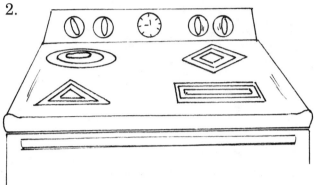

3.

4.

5.

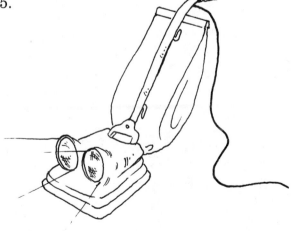

6.

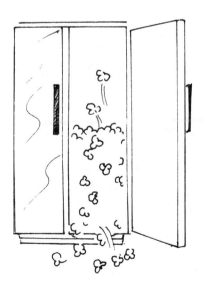

Would you buy any of these appliances? Tell why.

Let's Be Sensible!

Name _____

Read the sentences below. They don't make sense, do they? You can fix these sentences by using the names of the pictures instead of the underlined words. Write the letter of a picture above each underlined word so each sentence makes sense. Then, read your new, improved sentences!

1. I got some <u>feathers</u> at the bank.

    A.

2. I got the <u>dream</u> out of the garage.

    B.

3. I took a <u>saw</u> to the beach.

    C.

4. I saw a <u>flood</u> at the circus.

    D.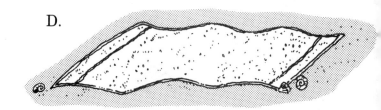

5. I like to <u>whisper</u> for my favorite football team.

    E.

Now, that makes sense!

Silly Sentences

Name _____

Read the silly sentences below. Then, draw a line to match the sentences with their pictures. Finally, tell why the sentences don't make sense.

1. Karen likes to eat nails.

2. We bought a plant at the theater.

3. I just finished painting the basketball.

4. Jerry reads the iron every evening.

5. I chose to have rainy weather today.

Make up your own silly sentence. Then, tell why it's silly.

Picture Match

Name _____

Find the pictures that go with these sentences. Write the letter of each picture beside the sentence it matches. Then, tell why the sentences don't make sense.

_____ 1. Jon smelled the cake with his beak.

A.

_____ 2. The child drove the cab to the airport.

B.

_____ 3. The man limped on his bad arm.

C.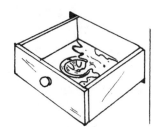

_____ 4. The pumpkin was wearing striped pajamas.

D.

_____ 5. The water went down the drain in the drawer.

E.

Change each sentence above so it makes sense. Then, write your own silly sentence and draw its picture on the back of this worksheet.

Fix Up

Name _____

Fix the sentences below so they make sense. Write a word from the box to replace the underlined word in each sentence.

bulldozer	smell	flower	frowned
meal	dollars	hare	celery
destroyed	wound	borrow	coast

1. I <u>coast</u> with my nose. _____

2. A <u>skunk</u> smells good. _____

3. The chef cooked a <u>tune</u>. _____

4. I like to eat <u>bread</u> raw. _____

5. We can <u>smell</u> on a sled. _____

6. The <u>buggy</u> knocked down one wall of the old building. _____

7. Jeremy owes me two <u>fingernails</u>. _____

8. I need to <u>lend</u> a pencil from Tim. _____

9. The workers <u>created</u> the old building. _____

10. Stacy <u>smiled</u> when she heard the sad news. _____

11. My dog has a <u>cellar</u> on his paw. _____

12. The <u>hive</u> sat quietly, eating grass. _____

You sure fixed those sentences!

Strange Crosswords!

Name _____

Finish the crossword puzzle with the words in the box below. Use the words in the box to replace the underlined words in the sentences.

enormous	emergency	deaf
earned	starved	council
damp	announced	cured

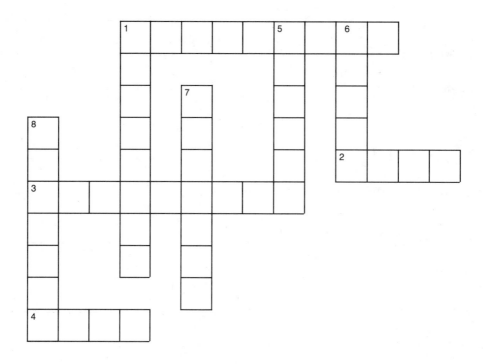

Across

1. Call the police if there's an <u>instant</u>.
2. The clothes in the dryer are still <u>homesick</u>.
3. Our teacher <u>borrowed</u> that we were having a math test.
4. He couldn't hear the bells because he's <u>blind</u>.

Down

1. That big rhinoceros is <u>electric</u>.
5. Sally <u>dialed</u> twenty dollars for babysitting overnight.
6. The operation <u>ruined</u> Dad's heart problem.
7. The city <u>banquet</u> meets once a month.
8. The wolf <u>squinted</u> because it couldn't find any food or water.

There's nothing strange about the way you handled this puzzle!

It's Your Draw

Name _____

Rewrite each sentence below so it makes sense. Then, draw a picture of your new sentences.

1. The plane arrived at the bus depot.

   _____

2. A bird uses its beak to swim.

   _____

3. I rode across the ocean in a cab.

   _____

Your new sentences make good sense!

Wrong Way!

Name _____

Read the sentences below. Then, tell what's wrong with each sentence.

1. My mom will carve the wood for Thanksgiving dinner.

2. A watermelon is greedy.

3. Jeff celebrated when he lost his camera.

4. You use a paintbrush to brush your teeth.

5. A hero lives in a cave.

6. We live in a house in the harbor.

Now, write answers to these questions about the words that made the sentences above sound silly.

7. What are three things you can carve?

   _____

8. Who can be greedy?

   _____

9. Name three things you might celebrate.

   _____

10. What do we use a paintbrush for?

   _____

11. Name two things that live in a cave.

   _____

12. What would you find in a harbor?

   _____

Now you're going the right way!

What a Pair!

Name _____

Read the pairs of sentences below. One sentence in each pair makes sense and the other one doesn't. Mark an X by each sentence that makes sense and an 0 by each one that doesn't.

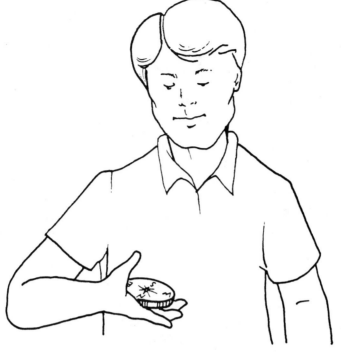

1. _____ I use a compass to find which direction I'm going.

   _____ I use a compass to measure my feet.

2. _____ My nightmare scared me.

   _____ My nightmare plays with me every night.

3. _____ I didn't eat the apple because it was rotten.

   _____ I didn't eat the apple because it tasted good.

4. _____ I enjoy riding in a sailboat on windy days.

   _____ I enjoy riding in a sailboat on the beach.

5. _____ I like cloudbursts because I get sunburned.

   _____ I like cloudbursts because I get wet.

6. _____ The beggar asked me to stay in his castle.

   _____ The beggar asked me for some money.

You made wise choices!

Tic-Tac-Toe

Name _____

Read the sentences below. Mark an X by the sentences that make sense and an 0 by the ones that don't. Be sure to read each sentence carefully!

1. _____ The leaky boat stayed afloat.

   _____ The leaky boat sank to the ocean floor.

   _____ The leaky boat filled up with water.

2. _____ Bold people are afraid to try new things.

   _____ Bold people have courage.

   _____ Bold people are usually shy.

3. _____ A furnace keeps a place warm.

   _____ A furnace cleans dirty dishes.

   _____ A furnace works a lot when it's cold outside.

4. _____ I used the whisk to play the piano.

   _____ I used the whisk to clean the cup.

   _____ I used the whisk to stir the mixture.

What's your next move in the tic-tac-toe game? You win!

You Don't Say!

Underline a word in each sentence below that doesn't make sense. Then, rewrite each sentence, using a word from the box.

valuable	colt	cookbook	avoid
acres	painful	crib	gardener

1. Jackie looked in her courtyard to find a good recipe for garlic chicken.

   _____

2. The ring was so worthless, Ben sold it for a thousand dollars.

   _____

3. The geologist planted the seeds by hand.

   _____

4. The new baby slept in a dungeon.

   _____

5. The large ranch has two hundred batches of land.

   _____

6. The horse's lasso stood on its wobbly legs.

   _____

7. Brent had to step on the brakes to recall hitting the car in front of him.

   _____

8. Dee's toothache felt very loyal.

   _____

Excellent work!

Crossword Capers

Name _____

Finish this crossword puzzle with the words in the box below. Use the words in the box to replace the underlined words in the sentences.

gumdrops	pedal	blizzard	nursery
trapeze	innocent	racket	snore
beef	custodian	commercial	

Across

1. The twist cleans the classrooms at the end of each day.
2. My favorite candy is cement.
3. You need a twitch to play tennis.
4. The baby slept in a chariot.
5. Some people magnify when they sleep.
6. We got stuck in a forecast in the mountains.

Down

1. We turn the channel when a hedge comes on.
6. The meat of a cow is called grub.
7. The defendant was found prickly.
8. It looks like fun to swing on a harpoon.
9. The boy had to clench faster to keep up with his dad.

You solved the puzzle!

Fool's Gold

Name _____

Don't let these sentences fool you! Rewrite each one so it makes sense.

1. Kara dawdles on her way to school, so she's always early.

   _____

 2. When I gain weight, I weigh less than before.

   _____

3. I like to hear Randy sing, so I ignore him.

   _____

4. Ray was the narrator of the story, so he didn't say much.

   _____

5. I prefer receiving an F grade instead of an A.

   _____

6. The tornado was unexpected after we heard the siren go off.

   _____

 7. The teacher praised the boy for his poor work.

   _____

8. We rode the trolley to the other side of the river.

   _____

You're not fooling around! These are great sentences!

What a Laugh!

Circle what's silly in these sentences. Then, write the correct sentence below the silly one.

1. I eat cereal every month for breakfast.

   _____

2. We saw a dolphin in the pet store aquarium.

   _____

3. The baseball player made a basket just before time ran out.

   _____

4. A centipede is a bicycle with many legs.

   _____

5. When its 100° outside, I turn the furnace on to keep warm.

   _____

6. When you throw a pass, you're playing a game of hopscotch.

   _____

7. One of the ingredients in pizza is macaroni.

   _____

8. During a hurricane, gentle winds blow.

   _____

9. We rode the ferry across the pond.

   _____

10. A baby pig is called a colt.

   _____

Do the sentences still sound silly? They hadn't butter!

This Sounds Silly!

Name _____

Explain why the sentences below sound silly. Then, write a correct sentence below each one.

1. The young giraffe already has tusks.

    _____

2. My uncle used a compass to mow his grass.

    _____

3. The table was so sturdy it collapsed.

    _____

4. The tractor's propeller wouldn't move.

    _____

5. The workers poured lumber to make new streets.

    _____

6. Sharon rides her sailboat on the sidewalk.

    _____

Thanks to you, the sentences aren't silly anymore!

Wrap It Up

Name _____

Choose words from the gift below to make each sentence make sense. Write the correct word above the underlined word in each sentence. Then, read the sentence again, using the new word.

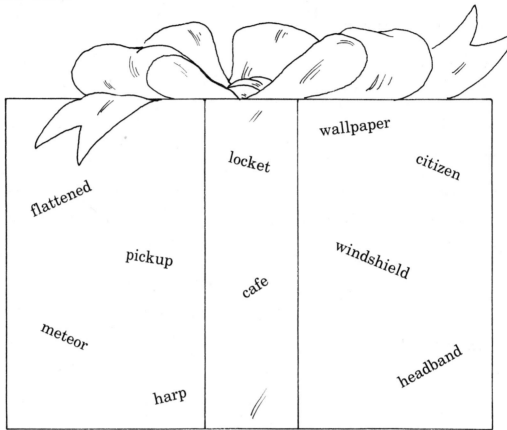

flattened
pickup
meteor
harp

locket
cafe

wallpaper
citizen
windshield
headband

1. I <u>simmered</u> the dough with the rolling pin.

2. We put up new <u>starch</u> in the kitchen.

3. Jean wears a <u>pretzel</u> around her neck.

4. The man threw the extra bales of hay into the <u>lab</u>.

5. Chan became a <u>trapper</u> of the United States last year.

6. We watched the <u>maze</u> fall out of sight.

7. The <u>parlor</u> makes a beautiful sound.

8. Juliet wears a <u>mattress</u> to keep her hair out of her face.

9. The <u>bracelet</u> of the car was covered with bugs.

10. Let's eat at the <u>dairy</u> today.

Good going!

Word Swap

Name _____

These sentences are all mixed up! The underlined words somehow got switched, so they're in the wrong sentences. Rewrite each sentence so it makes sense, using another underlined word on the page. Look at all the underlined words before you decide which one to use!

1. The king lives in a <u>drawbridge</u>.

_____

2. We went to the <u>skyscraper</u> to see the boxing match.

_____

3. The <u>shack</u> decided to begin the delicate operation.

_____

4. The soldier lifted the <u>refreshment</u> to keep the enemies out.

_____

5. The <u>arena</u> has ninety floors.

_____

6. The beggar's <u>castle</u> was falling apart.

_____

7. The basketball player needed some <u>jewels</u> after the tiring game.

_____

8. The woman keeps her expensive <u>surgeon</u> in a safe.

_____

Nice work on a hard task!

Tell Me Truthfully

Name _____

Look at the sentences below. Some of them make sense, but others don't. Circle a T for each sentence that's true and an F for each sentence that's false. Then, think how you can make each false sentence true. Write your new sentence below the old one.

T   F   1. A person can sit on a tree bough.

_____

T   F   2. You can cram furniture into a backpack.

_____

T   F   3. When you broil something, you freeze it.

_____

T   F   4. A menu is a list of food we can order.

_____

T   F   5. We sleep on pavement every night.

_____

T   F   6. Some people write in diaries every day.

_____

T   F   7. Petrified rock is soft and powdery.

_____

T   F   8. A fawn could arrest a robber.

_____

To tell the truth, you did very well!

Hot Fudge Sundae!

Name _____

Jim's hot fudge sundae didn't turn out quite right. Read the directions below to see how he made his sundae. Then, put a zero by each direction that Jim shouldn't have done when he made his sundae. Tell why those directions don't make sense.

1. _____ Put on an overcoat so you don't spill any ingredients on your clothes.

2. _____ Get a dish to put the ice cream in.

3. _____ Get a shovel from the cabinet.

4. _____ Take the ice cream out of the freezer.

5. _____ Broil the ice cream for ten minutes.

6. _____ Put several scoops of ice cream in the dish.

7. _____ Grate barbecue sauce on top of the ice cream.

8. _____ Sprinkle pears or limes on the ice cream.

9. _____ Use a lariat to open the hot fudge container.

10. _____ Pour hot fudge syrup over the ice cream.

11. _____ Measure a teaspoon of cherry.

12. _____ Place a cherry on top of your dessert.

13. _____ Use chopsticks to eat your yummy dessert!

14. _____ Place your sundae in front of you and devour!

Could you make a hot fudge sundae by only following the good directions above?

Change Up

Name _____

After each sentence below are three words. Circle the best word to replace the underlined word so the sentence makes sense. Then, read the sentence again with the correct word.

1. Alisha achieved perfection when she got every math problem <u>wrong</u>.

    legal, correct, persuaded

2. The barber will <u>mow</u> my hair.

    trim, expand, blot

3. The <u>mason</u> knew what was wrong as soon as he looked under the car's hood.

    orphan, sculptor, mechanic

4. Anna bought some <u>charcoal</u> to make a new skirt.

    fabric, adobe, morsels

5. The <u>pelican</u> raced to the scene of the accident.

    wheelbarrow, ambulance, bandit

6. We got stuck in a <u>wharf</u> as we drove home from our ski trip.

    rehearsal, courtroom, snowstorm

7. The <u>rudder</u> scurried to the other side of the barn.

    rodent, porridge, hoofbeats

8. The young boy's <u>gratitude</u> was very poor in school.

    frontier, pursuit, behavior

9. We use a puck to play <u>horseshoes</u>.

    dominoes, hockey, softball

10. The colt's legs were <u>sincere</u> when he tried to stand up.

    coarse, easygoing, wobbly

You changed every one! Nice work!

Cross-wise

Name _____

Read the sentences below and circle the words that don't make sense. Circle one word in each sentence. Then, look for those words in the word search puzzle!

1. Wait for the steak to ripen before you barbecue it.

2. I looked in the album to find my favorite casserole recipe.

3. We always buy our school supplies at the dairy.

4. Jason's tossed salad fell out of its bun.

5. There was a sour wind blowing last Friday.

6. Dad helped Mom navigate the seeds in the garden.

7. The wastebasket jumped to the top of the couch.

8. The waiter carefully poured the pizza into our glasses.

9. Julia wrapped herself in sandpaper to stay warm.

10. The distance from my house to the post office is three quarts.

W	T	C	P	I	Z	Z	A	R
A	T	M	J	K	N	Y	O	N
S	A	N	D	P	A	P	E	R
T	F	U	L	A	V	P	G	A
E	P	K	V	Y	I	H	O	L
B	U	H	J	R	G	R	W	B
A	Z	Q	W	S	A	D	Y	U
S	O	U	R	X	T	B	A	M
K	D	B	O	C	E	R	C	K
E	X	Q	U	A	R	T	S	H
T	L	Z	I	N	S	V	H	E

You're word wise! Now, say the sentences aloud, changing the circled words to make sense.

Trading Places

Read each sentence below. Then, circle the best word to replace the underlined word.

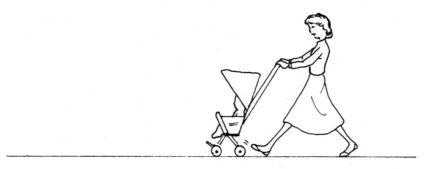

1. The new mother pushed the <u>mink</u> down the sidewalk.

    suitor   stroller   foal

2. The farmer used a <u>grinder</u> to toss hay to the animals.

    monarch   strainer   pitchfork

3. We'd better take an <u>ideal</u> route since this one is blocked.

    enthusiastic   outlandish   alternate

4. The truck driver had to stop at the <u>serenade</u>.

    tollbooth   mantel   observatory

5. The <u>plankton</u> spread its feathers into a beautiful fan.

    varmint   jellyfish   peacock

6. Joyce poured the liquid through the <u>muzzle</u>.

    fortress   funnel   igloo

7. When you have broken the law, you've done something <u>ambitious</u>.

    illegal   forlorn   drab

8. Please put the dirty saucepans and spoons in the <u>collage</u>.

    dishwasher   cornmeal   sanctuary

You made some good trades!

Patch-work

Name _____

Circle a word in each sentence that doesn't make sense. Then, replace it with a word from the box below. Write your new sentences below the old ones. The silly sentences will be patched up in no time!

dinosaur	yacht	exam
bushel	shuttle	postcard

1. The submarine took the astronauts to their spacecraft.

    _____

2. Last year, we took our summer vacation on a barge.

    _____

3. A triceratops is a kind of hippopotamus.

    _____

4. I got a factor in the mail from my cousin.

    _____

5. Judy has a math laser next Tuesday.

    _____

6. We gathered a nectar of apples from one tree.

    _____

You do amazing work!

That's Absurd!

Name _____

Read the sentences below. Then, fix the sentences so they make sense. Write your new sentences below the old ones. There may be more than one way to fix each sentence!

1. The incense had a petrified smell.

    _____

2. Mom wrote a check to cancel our tickets for the play.

    _____

3. The detective bleached the investigation when he caught the thief.

    _____

4. My savings account grew when I withdrew money from it.

    _____

5. In the summer, we usually get a lot of sleet.

    _____

6. The piano solo was so good that the audience didn't applaud.

    _____

7. Karen was a passenger in the hospital for two weeks after her car accident.

    _____

8. When Andrew's stereo blared, his neighbors never heard it.

    _____

Now, make up your own absurd sentence. Tell why your sentence is absurd. Then, change it so it makes sense!

School Days

Name _____

Read the story below. It tells about a boy named Jon. Underline one sentence in each paragraph that doesn't make sense. When you're finished, read the story again, but fix the underlined sentences so they make sense.

Jon was absent from school every day last year, so he got a perfect attendance award. He never missed a single day! He was very proud of his award.

Jon's favorite subject in school is math. Last year, Jon learned about addition and subtraction. This year, he'll learn about disposal and division. Someday, he'd like to be a math teacher.

Jon also enjoys reading class. He likes to read nonfiction stories. Nonfiction fascinates Jon because he knows what he's reading isn't true.

At the end of each day, Jon volunteers to help his teacher. He usually washes the erasers and sweeps the chalkboard. Sometimes, he straightens up the bookshelves. The teacher really appreciates his help.

When he gets home, Jon smears his homework. He rereads his lessons for the day and writes down any questions he has. Then, he's all ready for another day of school!

What's your favorite subject in school?

Dictionary Disgrace

Name _____

The editors of this dictionary must have been in a hurry! Look at the definitions below to see what I mean. See if you can switch the words around to match the correct definitions. Cross out the old words and write the correct ones below them.

1. abbreviation • a promise or agreement

   _____

2. fatigued • having great joy

   _____

3. griddle • a beautiful gem, usually deep blue

   _____

4. jubilant • extremely important

   _____

5. persist • to become married

   _____

6. pledge • a shortened form of a written word or phrase

   _____

7. salary • a flat, metal surface or pan to cook food on

   _____

8. sapphire • a fixed amount of money paid for work done

   _____

9. vital • being extremely tired from labor or physical activity

   _____

10. wed • to continue doing something for a long time

   _____

Maybe you should be an editor!

Crossword Comedy

Name _____

Finish this crossword puzzle with the words in the box below. Use the words in the box to replace the underlined words in the sentences.

swiveled	spectator	revived	denim
juvenile	spat	tropical	bleach
foes	chaos	somber	

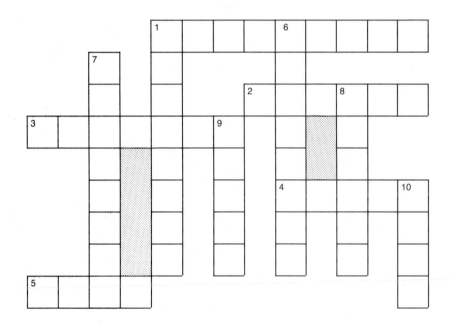

Across

1. I prefer not to play sports, but to be a <u>participant</u>.
2. Everyone's faces were <u>parallel</u> when they heard of the tragedy.
3. Tyler <u>meshed</u> the infant after it fell into the pond.
4. There was <u>charity</u> when the animals got loose in the zoo.
5. The enemies had been <u>chums</u> since the war started.

Down

1. June <u>furrowed</u> around in her chair.
6. I'd like to visit a <u>mobile</u> island where it's always warm.
7. If you're seventeen or younger, you're considered a <u>parent</u>.
8. I use <u>ore</u> to keep my white clothes white.
9. My blue jeans are made of <u>twine</u>.
10. After their <u>migration</u>, Greg and Lois apologized to each other.

Thanks for a good laugh!

Antonyms

Children are taught antonyms throughout the school curriculum. As the grade level increases, curricular words become more difficult and abstract. As children get older, they're able to understand the meaning of the abstract vocabulary and by making a quick translation to a more concrete meaning, they can identify a word with the opposite meaning.

The language-delayed child may have difficulty with antonyms for a number of reasons. First, he may not focus on the critical semantic feature that must be changed in order to form a word with the opposite meaning. For example, the child who says "big" is the opposite of "narrow" is not focusing on the critical semantic feature of width, but rather on the element of size. Second, the child may not have the specific vocabulary skills necessary to give the correct answer. He may have an internal understanding of the critical semantic element of the word, but he may not have the specific word in his lexicon to express the opposite. Or, he may not know the meaning of a word, and therefore cannot give its opposite. Third, the child may not possess the process for determining opposites. He may not know that one critical feature of the target word and its opposite must be reversed. Finally, the child may have word-retrieval problems and be unable to express the antonym.

These Antonyms worksheets focus on the identification of words with opposite meanings, providing a base on which to build an understanding of more complex vocabulary. Your students will learn they need to be precise in naming opposites. For example, the opposite of "cold," or the total absence of heat, must be "hot," the total absence of cold; "warm" isn't close enough. Your students will also learn that antonyms, like synonyms, must be expressed in a single word, and that not all words have exact opposites.

Antonyms

133

Short or Tall?

Look at these pictures. Color the tall things red. Color the short things blue. Tall and short are opposites!

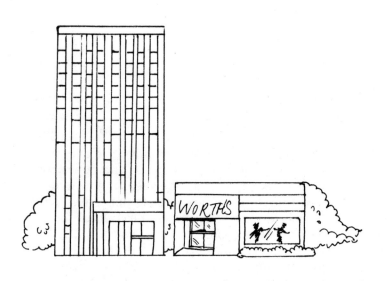

Are you short or tall?

Happy or Sad?

Draw a frown on one face. Draw a smile on the other face. Then, add some hair to finish your pictures. Do the faces look the same now?

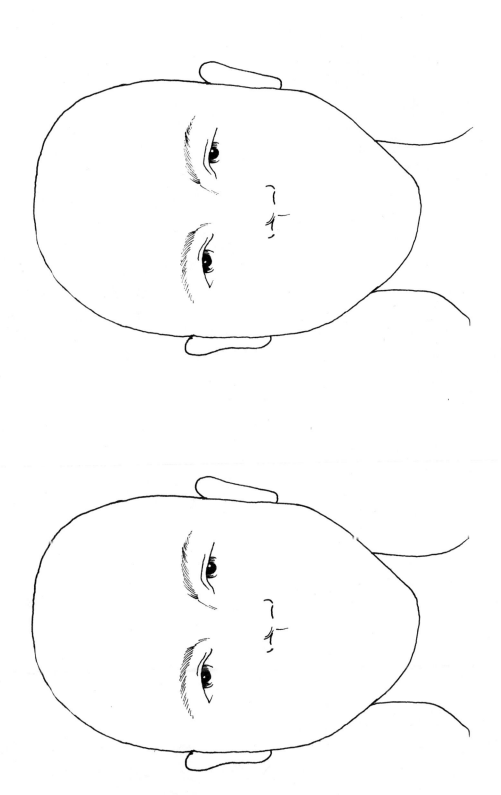

Look in a mirror. Do you have a smile or a frown on your face?

135

Quiet or Noisy?

Name _____

Draw a circle around the things that are quiet. Draw a line under the things that are noisy.

1.

2.

3.

4.

5.

6.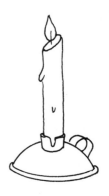

7.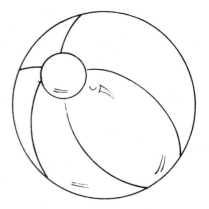

8.

What can you do that makes noise?

Make a Choice

Look at the pictures below. Then, circle the answer to each question.

1. It's Ian's birthday. What will he do?   give presents   get presents

2. This yo-yo doesn't work. What will Dad do?   fix it   break it

3. Ken wants to tell a secret. What will he do?   yell   whisper

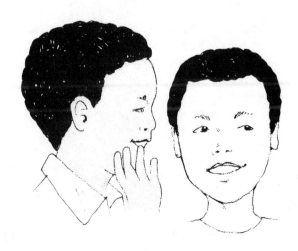

What's special about telling a secret?

Alike or Different?

Circle the pictures that are alike in each row. Draw an X on the picture that is different.

1.

2.

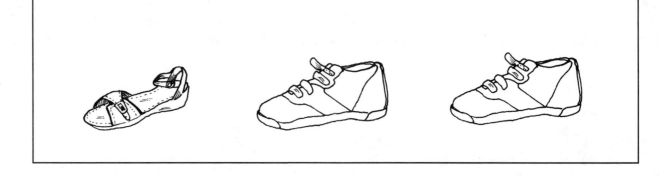

3.

4.

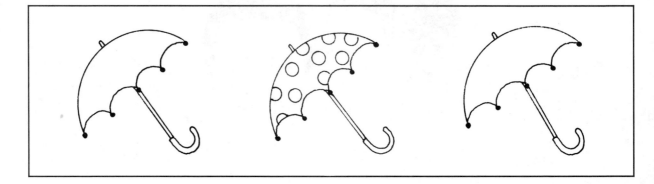

Are your eyes alike or different? How about your feet?

Lots of Lines

Name _____

Read the directions below, then do what they say. Read carefully!

1. Draw a straight line in this box.

2. Draw a crooked line in this box.

3. Draw a long line in this box.

4. Draw a short line in this box.

5. Draw a line below this bird.

6. Draw a line above this bird.

You're in line for success!

Cactus Facts

Name _____

How does a cactus grow in a desert? Read the paragraph below to find out! Fill in each blank with a word that is the opposite of the word below the blank. Choose words from the box.

dry	thin	desert
near	deserts	best
outside	catch	thick

Cacti grow in very _____ areas called _____ . How do
               1. wet   2. swamps

they get enough water? Their roots are very _____ to the ground
                                         3. far

surface, so they can _____ rainwater. Also, their roots have a special
                    4. throw

covering on the _____ that holds water. Cacti have very
                 5. inside

_____ leaves, or needles, and they have very _____ stems
    6. thick   7. thin

that can hold a lot of water. There may not be much rain in a _____ ,
                                             8. swamp

but the cactus plant makes the _____ use of the water it gets.
                           9. worst

How could you use a cactus to survive in the desert?

Munch, Munch!

Some foods are soft, and some foods are crunchy. Draw a line to match each food to the right box. The first one is done for you.

1. applesauce ————

2. bread stick

3. marshmallow

4. potato chips

5. pretzels

```
┌─────────────────┐
│                 │
│      SOFT       │
│                 │
└─────────────────┘

┌─────────────────┐
│                 │
│    CRUNCHY      │
│                 │
└─────────────────┘
```

6. pudding

7. raw carrots

8. yogurt

9. strawberry

10. raw celery

What are your favorite foods? Are they soft or crunchy? Write the names of three of your favorite foods below and tell why you like each one.

favorite food

11. _____   I like it because _____

_____

12. _____   I like it because _____

_____

13. _____   I like it because _____

_____

How do you fix your favorite food? Tell me all about it!

It's Your Choice!

Name _____

People like different things. Put a check mark beside the object you'd rather have from each pair listed below. Then, we'll know what you like!

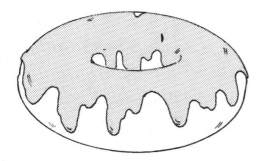 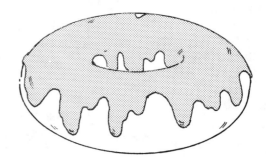

Which would you rather have?

1.	_____ a stale doughnut	_____ a fresh doughnut	
2.	_____ a cool drink	_____ a warm drink	
3.	_____ an empty pop bottle	_____ a full pop bottle	
4.	_____ a heavy backpack	_____ a light backpack	
5.	_____ a sharp knife	_____ a dull knife	
6.	_____ a soft pillow	_____ a hard pillow	
7.	_____ straight hair	_____ curly hair	
8.	_____ a wide belt	_____ a narrow belt	
9.	_____ a summer vacation	_____ a winter vacation	

Now, tell why you checked each one.

Match These Opposites

Name _____

Draw a line to match each word with its opposite. The first one is done for you.

1. beautiful   cold

2. clean   far

3. hot   dry

4. wet   ugly

5. near   dirty

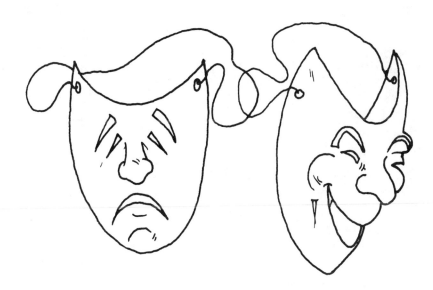

Circle Yes or No to answer each question.

6. Are flowers ugly?   Yes   No

7. Is a milk shake cold?   Yes   No

8. Is the sun far away?   Yes   No

9. Is a new shirt dirty?   Yes   No

10. Is this paper wet?   Yes   No

Draw two Halloween masks on the back of this paper. Make one beautiful and one ugly. Which one do you like better?

Crazy Computer

Name _____

Uh-oh! Ben tried to write a thank-you letter to his aunt, but his computer didn't work right. It printed the opposite of what Ben wanted to say. Help Ben rewrite the letter. Write the opposite of the underlined words in the blanks on the right. Look at the words in the box below if you need help.

buy	glad	after	love	wonderful
friends	new	sending	Aunt	tomorrow
my	fine	nephew	thank you	day

1.
Dear Uncle Nancy,

       2.   3.
Thank you for receiving me the money for your

       4.
birthday. I was sad to hear from you.

       5.
I used the money to sell a baseball mitt. My

6.   7.   8.
enemies and I hate to play baseball before school

       9.   10.
every night. I can hardly wait to use my old mitt

11.
yesterday!

               12.   13.
I hope you are feeling awful. You're welcome

               14.
for the birthday present. It's terrible!

               15.
Your niece,

      Ben

1. _____
2. _____
3. _____
4. _____
5. _____
6. _____
7. _____
8. _____
9. _____
10. _____
11. _____
12. _____
13. _____
14. _____
15. _____

Now, write a letter to your own relative. Think of something interesting to say!

What's Special about Siberia?

Name _____

Fill in the blanks below to find out some interesting facts about Siberia. Write the opposite of the word below each blank so the paragraph makes sense. Use the words in the box to help you.

first	cold	fresh	lowest
coldest	good	below	cold
healthy	northern	always	

Siberia is in the _____ part of the Soviet Union. It is
        1. southern

_____ cold in Siberia. It is one of the _____ places
2. never   3. hottest

people live in the world. The _____ temperature ever recorded in
                                4. highest

Siberia was 90° _____ zero. That's _____ !
                    5. above   6. hot

There are two _____ things about living in Siberia.
                 7. bad

_____ , food stays _____ a long time. Second, it's too
8. Last   9. stale

_____ for germs, so people stay _____ most of the time!
10. hot   11. sick

What sports could people play in Siberia? Where would they play them?

Opposites Attract

Tim and Ron are best friends, but they do everything the opposite way! Choose a word from the box to finish each sentence.

follow	sour	plain	slower	right
dull	send	late	straight	spends

1. When Tim walks faster, Ron walks _____ .

2. Tim likes curly hair, but Ron likes _____ hair.

3. Tim likes to be early, but Ron like to be _____ .

4. When Tim turns left, Ron turns _____ .

5. Tim saves his money, but Ron _____ his money.

6. Tim likes sweet foods, but Ron likes _____ foods.

7. Tim likes to receive letters, but Ron likes to _____ them.

8. Tim likes to use sharp pencils, but Ron likes to use _____ ones.

9. Tim likes fancy cupcakes, but Ron likes _____ cupcakes.

10. Tim likes to lead, but Ron likes to _____ .

What do you do that's the opposite of what your best friend does?

146

Which Melts Faster?

Name _____

Which melts faster, clean snow or dirty snow? Write the opposite of the word below each blank to fill in the missing information. Then, read the paragraph to find out which kind of snow melts faster.

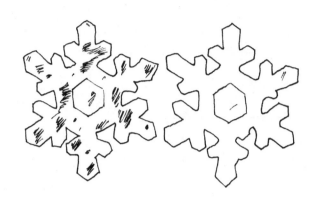

Does _____ snow melt _____ than dirty snow?
       1. dirty   2. slower

_____ snow is _____ ice crystals that reflect light, so
   3. Dirty   4. melted

they look _____ . These _____ crystals send the
          5. black   6. black

_____ rays back into the air. _____ snow is
   7. dark   8. Clean

_____ , so it collects more heat from the sun. The heat makes the dirty
   9. light

snow _____ _____ than clean snow. So,
    10. freeze   11. slower

_____ snow _____ faster than _____ snow!
   12. clean   13. freezes   14. dirty

Why do we wear light clothes in the summer and dark clothes in the winter?

Do the Opposite!

Name _____

We usually follow what directions say to do. Here's your chance to do the opposite!
Read each direction carefully. Then, do the opposite on your worksheet. Pay close
attention to the underlined words for clues. Have fun!

1. Write your name <u>beneath</u> the star.

2. Draw an X <u>inside</u> the star.

3. Color the shape on the <u>left</u>.

4. Draw a circle at the <u>top</u> of the page.

5. Draw a square at the <u>bottom</u> of the page.

6. Trace the outline of the shape on the <u>right</u>.

7. Draw a <u>sad</u> face beside your name.

Now, make your own worksheet with crazy directions. Let a friend have fun following
your mixed-up directions!

Choices, Choices!

Name _____

Circle the answer to each question. Pick the best choice!

1. Is a wrestler weak or strong?   weak   strong

2. Is a park public or private?   public   private

3. Is a dancer graceful or clumsy?   graceful   clumsy

4. Is a stranger unknown or familiar?   unknown   familiar

5. Is a peacock dull or colorful?   dull   colorful

6. Does an inventor create or destroy things?   create   destroy

Now, you get to be creative! The make-believe machine below creates animals for zoos in outer space. Draw an animal the machine made. Make it colorful! Then, tell how the machine made your animal.

You made some colorful choices!

Sense and Nonsense

Name _____

Read the sentence pairs below. Then, put a check mark beside each sentence that makes sense. The sentence pairs have the opposite meanings.

1. _____ A dragon is make-believe.

   _____ A dragon is real.

2. _____ An ocean is shallow.

   _____ An ocean is deep.

3. _____ A football field is narrow.

   _____ A football field is wide.

4. _____ A candle is solid.

   _____ A candle is hollow.

5. _____ We reward criminals.

   _____ We punish criminals.

6. _____ Lightning is visible.

   _____ Lightning is invisible.

7. _____ A whisper is noisy.

   _____ A whisper is quiet.

8. _____ A brick sinks in water.

   _____ A brick floats in water.

9. _____ A pencil is crooked.

   _____ A pencil is straight.

10. _____ A diamond is shiny.

    _____ A diamond is dull.

Did you make some sense out of this?

Silly Seth

Name _____

Seth is silly. He does everything backwards! Choose a word from the box to finish each sentence. Find out why Seth is silly!

disobeys	rapidly	subtracts	playful	spends
right	frowns	nervous	lie	yells

1. When Seth should smile, he _____ .

2. When Seth should add, he _____ .

3. When Seth should save, he _____ .

4. When Seth should whisper, he _____ .

5. When Seth should behave, he _____ .

6. When Seth should be calm, he's _____ .

7. When Seth should be serious, he's _____ .

8. When Seth should turn left, he turns _____ .

9. When Seth should tell the truth, he tells a _____ .

10. When Seth should do something slowly, he does it _____ .

Say this three times quickly: Seth does silly things.

Isn't that silly?

What's It All About?

Name _____

Put a check mark in the blank beside the opposite meaning for each word or phrase.

1. The opposite of *faraway* is

   _____ in the distance.

   _____ nearby.

   _____ away from here.

2. The opposite of the *farthest house* is

   _____ the faraway house.

   _____ the largest house.

   _____ the nearest house.

3. The opposite of *at dawn* is

   _____ at sunset.

   _____ at sunrise.

   _____ at noon.

4. The opposite of *northern* is

   _____ eastern.

   _____ western.

   _____ southern.

5. The opposite of *outer edge* is

   _____ in the center.

   _____ at the side.

   _____ along the edge.

How do phrases like "outer edge" help us communicate?

Crossword Opposites

Name _____

Use the words in the box to help you do this crossword puzzle.

narrow	wife	dangerous	leader	sun	modern
truth	false	wonderful	upper	float	

Across

1. the opposite of husband
2. the opposite of shade
3. the opposite of safe
4. the opposite of lower
5. the opposite of true
6. the opposite of sink
7. the opposite of wide

Down

1. the opposite of terrible
8. the opposite of old-fashioned
9. the opposite of a lie
10. the opposite of follower

You did the opposite of poorly!

Opposites!

Name _____

Choose the correct word to finish each sentence about opposites. Write the answers in the blanks.

1. Fierce is the opposite of _____ .   shallow   gentle   wild

2. Smile is the opposite of _____ .   frown   laugh   grin

3. Famous is the opposite of _____ .   familiar   new   unknown

4. Crisp is the opposite of _____ .   crunchy   soggy   fresh

5. Plain is the opposite of _____ .   nervous   dull   fancy

6. Delicate is the opposite of _____ .   sturdy   weak   fragile

7. Feast is the opposite of _____ .   meal   desert   famine

8. Hollow is the opposite of _____ .   solid   tough   round

9. Least is the opposite of _____ .   few   most   less

10. Shallow is the opposite of _____ .   low   clear   deep

Wonderful work!

No Nonsense!

These sentences don't make sense! Rewrite each sentence. Change the underlined word to an opposite word from the box so the sentence makes sense.

dangerous	aloud	difference	true
encourage	dawn	difficult	proud

1. The teacher read <u>silently</u> to his class.

   _____

2. Phil is <u>ashamed</u> of the award he won for his hard work.

   _____

3. It's <u>safe</u> to look at the sun without wearing sunglasses.

   _____

4. We'll leave at <u>dusk</u> so we can travel all day.

   _____

5. Threading a needle is <u>easy</u> if you can't see well.

   _____

6. There's not much <u>similarity</u> between two eggs.

   _____

7. Compliments usually <u>discourage</u> people.

   _____

8. A fact is <u>false</u> information about something.

   _____

No doubt about it. You did very well!

Match 'em Up!

Name _____

Read the words in each box. Draw lines to match the words that go together. The first box is started for you.

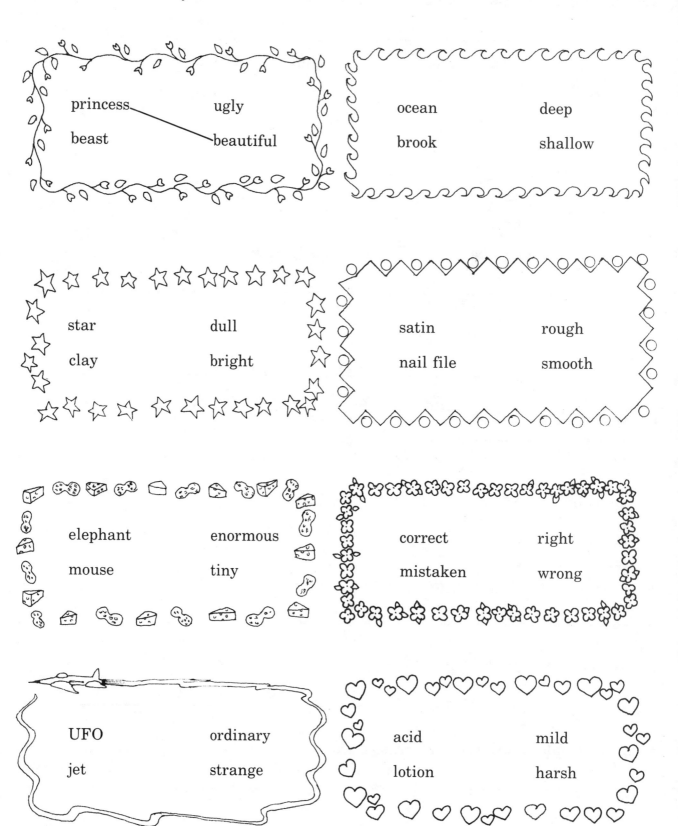

princess — beautiful

beast   ugly

ocean   deep

brook   shallow

star   dull

clay   bright

satin   rough

nail file smooth

elephant enormous

mouse   tiny

correct   right

mistaken wrong

UFO   ordinary

jet   strange

acid   mild

lotion   harsh

Nice matching!

Crossword Fun!

Name _____

Use the words in the box to help you do this crossword puzzle.

left	evening	outside	below	brother
front	together	ahead	ugly	remember

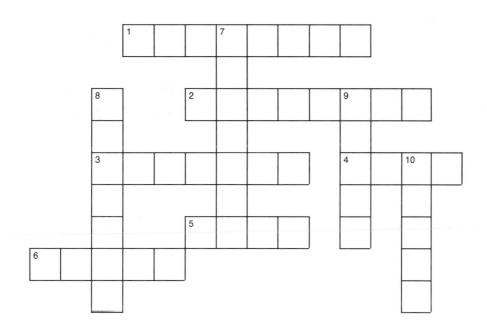

Across

1. the opposite of apart
2. the opposite of forget
3. the opposite of inside
4. the opposite of right
5. the opposite of beautiful
6. the opposite of behind

Down

7. the opposite of morning
8. the opposite of sister
9. the opposite of above
10. the opposite of back

Could you make your own crossword puzzle? Go ahead and try!

What's the Meaning of This?

Put a check mark in the blank beside the opposite meaning for each word or phrase.

1. The opposite of *read it aloud* is

   _____ read it silently.

   _____ read it loudly.

   _____ read it carefully.

2. The opposite of *in shallow water* is

   _____ where the water isn't deep.

   _____ where the water is clear.

   _____ where the water is deep.

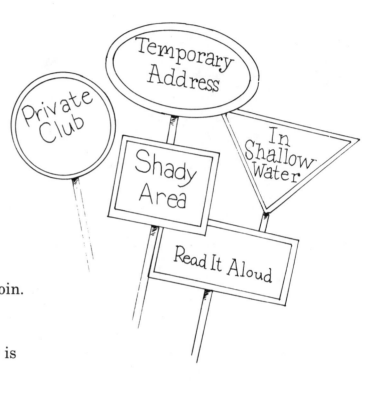

3. The opposite of *a private club* is

   _____ a club no one can join.

   _____ a club anyone can join.

   _____ a club people are invited to join.

4. The opposite of a *temporary address* is

   _____ an address for a short time.

   _____ a permanent address.

   _____ a business address.

5. The opposite of a *shady area* is

   _____ a sunny place.

   _____ a cool place.

   _____ a rainy place.

Now I know what you mean!

Sunken Treasure

Name _____

Be a treasure hunter! Draw a diving path to connect the opposites for the words in the boxes on the left.

1. | reward | admire   praise   punish

2. | joyful | elated   sad   happy

3. | nervous | harm   calm   excited

4. | attack | defend   war   fight

5. | familiar | unknown   known   famous

6. | feast | breakfast   famine   dinner

7. | neat | tidy   clean   messy

8. | crisp | crunchy   soggy   brittle

9. | hollow | solid   empty   open

10. | front | entrance   rear   middle

What do you think is inside the chest? Draw your answer on the back of this sheet.

The Frogfish

Name _____

Fill in the opposite of the word below each blank to finish this paragraph about the frogfish. Find out what makes a frogfish special!

catches	floats	long	tiny	end
smaller	outside	rare	prey	

A frogfish is a _____ animal because of the way it _____
                           1. common   2. throws

its food. It grows _____ threads on the _____ of its
                       3. short   4. inside

head that look like fishing lines. Each thread has a barb, or hook, at the

_____ . While the frogfish waits for its _____ , it
   5. beginning   6. friends

_____ its threads in the water. _____ fish think these
    7. sinks   8. Larger

threads are worms. When these _____ fish nibble on the threads, the
                                 9. huge

fish are hooked. The frogfish really knows how to fish!

How is a frogfish like a frog? How is it different?

Take Your Pick!

Choose the best word to finish each sentence. Write your answers in the blanks.

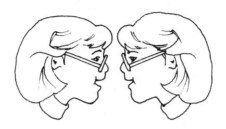

1. Identical twins look very _____ .

    similar   different

2. _____ the lid to keep the food fresh.

    Loosen   Tighten

3. Use a _____ cleaning solution to protect the car's finish.

    mild   harsh

4. We fell asleep during the _____ campaign speech.

    brief   lengthy

5. If there's a fire, head for the _____ exit.

    nearest   farthest

6. _____ people don't tell lies.

    Honest   Dishonest

7. Poison is _____ .

    harmless   harmful

8. Water is _____ in a drought.

    scarce   plentiful

9. Zoos try to _____ different kinds of animals.

    endanger   protect

10. The _____ is the one who pays for something.

    seller   buyer

What would you like and dislike about having an identical twin?

Choose Your Opposites

Choose the correct word to finish each sentence about opposites. Write the answers in the blanks.

1. The opposite of reward is   honor   punish   praise
   _____ .

2. The opposite of shady is   cloudy   sunny   foggy
   _____ .

3. The opposite of refuse is   send   deny   accept
   _____ .

4. The opposite of sloppy is   tidy   careless   messy
   _____ .

5. The opposite of serious is   playful   sad   honest
   _____ .

6. The opposite of protect is   lend   keep   harm
   _____ .

7. The opposite of rare is   unusual   common   true
   _____ .

8. The opposite of harden is   soften   fasten   listen
   _____ .

9. The opposite of prevent is   stop   cure   cause
   _____ .

10. The opposite of success is   failure   victory   prize
    _____ .

Terrific answers!

You Be the Judge!

Name _____

Read each question. Choose the correct underlined word to answer each question. Write your answers in the blanks. The first one is done for you.

1. Is a stranger someone <u>familiar</u> or <u>unfamiliar</u>? ___unfamiliar_____

2. Is a solution a <u>question</u> or an <u>answer</u>? _____

3. Is a stout animal <u>thin</u> or <u>fat</u>? _____

4. Is an antique vase <u>sturdy</u> or <u>brittle</u>? _____

5. Is rain in a desert <u>scarce</u> or <u>plentiful</u>? _____

6. Is a bold person <u>brave</u> or <u>timid</u>? _____

7. Does a forest fire <u>protect</u> or <u>endanger</u> animals? _____

8. Is a short speech <u>lengthy</u> or <u>brief</u>? _____

9. Do you <u>descend</u> or <u>ascend</u> to go uphill? _____

10. Does a forecast tell about the <u>future</u> or the <u>past</u>? _____

11. Is a clumsy person <u>graceful</u> or <u>awkward</u>? _____

12. Is something done on purpose <u>accidental</u> or <u>planned</u>? _____

If you don't know the answers to these questions right away, how can you find out?

Leaping Opposites

Leap across Bullfrog's Pond in just ten leaps. Each time you find the opposite of the word listed, write the number of that word on the lily pad. The first one is done for you. Happy leaping!

1. thick
2. worst
3. villain
4. husband
5. make-believe
6. tame
7. straighten
8. harden
9. private

Now, name the opposite of each word on the lily pads. Hop to it!

Crazy Cooking!

Name _____

Yikes! These recipe directions need your help! Write the opposite of each numbered word in the blank on the right. The answers are in the box on the left. The first one is done for you.

smooth
combine
warm
heat
gently
large
wet
melts
top
soft
add
half
divide
rise
dry
cool
sharp
boils

1.
Cool the milk until it almost freezes.
3.
Subtract the butter to the milk. Stir
4.
until the butter freezes.

5.   6.   7.
Separate the wet ingredients in a small
8.
bowl. Use a dull knife to blend the

mixture.

9.
Add the dry ingredients to the flour
10.
mixture. Stir roughly until the mixture
11.   12.
makes a hard, lumpy dough.

13.   14.
Multiply the dough in whole. Shape each

part into a ball and put in baking pans.
15.   16.
Let the dough fall in a cool place until it

doubles in size.

17.
Bake each loaf at 375° until the bottom is
18.
lightly browned. Heat each loaf on a

wire rack.

1. __Heat__

2. _____

3. _____

4. _____

5. _____

6. _____

7. _____

8. _____

9. _____

10. _____

11. _____

12. _____

13. _____

14. _____

15. _____

16. _____

17. _____

18. _____

What does this recipe make? What would happen if you tried to follow the directions without changing them?

ANTONYMS   165   Copyright © 1988 LinguiSystems, Inc.

Match the Opposites

Match each word to its opposite. Write the letter of the opposite word in the blank. The first one is done for you.

1. __A__ abrupt

2. ____ visible

3. ____ cease

4. ____ defend

5. ____ doubtful

6. ____ genuine

7. ____ hardy

8. ____ reveal

9. ____ oppose

A. gradual

B. sudden

C. invisible

D. hide

E. certain

F. real

G. lighten

H. unknown

I. obvious

J. protect

K. attack

L. agree

M. stop

N. strong

O. begin

P. frail

Q. show

R. fake

Now, fill in the correct letter in each of the spaces below. The first one is done for you. When you are done, you will find the answer to this question:

What do you get if you mix a poodle, a rooster, and a cocker spaniel?

A
‾‾ ‾‾ ‾‾ ‾‾ ‾‾ ‾‾ ‾‾   ‾‾ ‾‾ ‾‾ ‾‾ ‾‾ ‾‾   ‾‾ ‾‾
1   2 3 2 4 5 6   7 3 3 8 9 5   8 3

Find the Opposite

Name _____

Choose the correct word to finish each sentence about opposites. Write the answers in the blanks.

1. Attic is the opposite of

   _____ .

   ceiling   kitchen   basement

2. Student is the opposite of

   _____ .

   teacher   pupil   child

3. Accept is the opposite of

   _____ .

   receive   reject   lend

4. Freeze is the opposite of

   _____ .

   chill   melt   cool

5. Feeble is the opposite of

   _____ .

   strong   weak   frail

6. Purchase is the opposite of

   _____ .

   buy   locate   sell

7. Permanent is the opposite of

   _____ .

   temporary   new   used

8. Criticize is the opposite of

   _____ .

   promise   blame   praise

9. Plus is the opposite of

   _____ .

   minus   more   few

10. Anxious is the opposite of

    _____ .

    tense   scared   calm

You found all the opposites!

Do You Have a Match?

Name _____

Match each word to its opposite. Write the letter of the opposite word in the blank.

1. _____ poverty

2. _____ combine

3. _____ drought

4. _____ defeat

5. _____ expensive

6. _____ knowledge

7. _____ mourn

8. _____ native

a.	celebrate
b.	cheap
c.	wealth
d.	arrest
e.	flood
f.	information
g.	foreign
h.	national
i.	blend
j.	ignorance
k.	separate
l.	victory

Now, finish these sentences using words from the box.

9. The _____ victims had to flee their homes by boat.

10. Use a hand mixer to _____ the ingredients.

11. I'd like to travel to _____ countries.

12. It's hard to _____ an egg with one hand.

13. The eagle is the _____ bird of the United States.

14. We saw the police officer _____ the bank robber.

You matched the words up very well!

Make It Make Sense!

Name _____

These sentences need help! Replace each underlined word with its opposite word from the box. Then, rewrite each sentence so it makes sense.

loosen	celebrate	lengthen	weary
shrink	fertile	arrest	fresh

1. Many trees and plants grew quickly in the <u>barren</u> land.

   _____

2. The police officer came quickly to <u>release</u> the burglar at our house.

   _____

3. Buy the larger shirt because it might <u>expand</u> when you wash it.

   _____

4. I love the smell of <u>stale</u> bread baking in the oven!

   _____

5. Cindy grew two inches this summer, so she has to <u>shorten</u> her skirts.

   _____

6. We felt <u>rested</u> after the long, hard climb.

   _____

7. Joe had to <u>tighten</u> his belt after eating such a big dinner.

   _____

8. I'm having a party to <u>mourn</u> my birthday!

   _____

Now, that makes sense!

Support Your Choice!

Name _____

Answer these questions about opposites. Then, tell why you chose your answers.

Here's an example:

Would you rather see a comedy or a tragedy at the theater?

I'd rather see a comedy because I like to laugh. _____

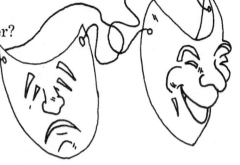

1. Would you rather buy a new car or a used car?

   _____

2. Do you prefer pictures with a glossy finish or a dull finish?

   _____

3. Would you rather be the oldest or the youngest in your family?

   _____

4. When you go swimming, do you like to get into the water suddenly or gradually?

   _____

5. Would you rather see a brief movie or a lengthy movie?

   _____

6. Would you rather gain weight or lose weight?

   _____

7. Would you rather eat raw carrots or cooked carrots?

   _____

8. Would you rather watch a sunrise or a sunset?

   _____

Would you rather write a letter or draw a picture? Show your answer on the back of this sheet.

Sentence Sense

Choose the correct word from the box to finish each sentence below.

hero	niece	pedestrian	restrain	urban
nephew	passenger	release	rural	villain

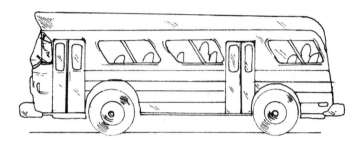

1. Each _____ paid a fare to ride the bus.

2. My sister's son is my _____ .

3. The evil _____ never cared about anyone but himself.

4. _____ areas have lots of traffic and many stores.

5. My sister's daughter is my _____ .

6. The heavy chains helped to _____ the eager spectators.

7. We stopped our car to let a _____ cross the street.

8. My cousin grew up on a farm in a _____ area of Ohio.

9. We will _____ the balloons after the victory speech.

10. Ben was a brave _____ who saved our lives during the fire.

What did you notice about the words in the box? Find the five pairs of opposites and write them on the back of this sheet.

Double Your Answers!

Name _____

Read each question. Then, underline your answer.

1. Is a one-hundred-year-old chair antique or new?	antique	new
2. Does a salesclerk purchase or sell things?	purchase	sell
3. Does the *X* sign mean you divide or multiply?	divide	multiply
4. Is the top of a table horizontal or vertical?	horizontal	vertical
5. Is a wet noodle crisp or soggy?	crisp	soggy
6. Does the sun appear or disappear at sunset?	appear	disappear
7. Is a spotlight dim or bright?	dim	bright
8. Is a cobweb delicate or sturdy?	delicate	sturdy
9. Do we use a lamp to brighten or darken a room?	brighten	darken
10. Does an artist create or destroy a painting?	create	destroy

Now, use the words you underlined to finish these sentences.

11. Too much milk can make cereal _____ .

12. The cleaner made the ink spot _____ .

13. I'd like to _____ a new kind of travel for outer space.

14. We're gathering the things we want to _____ at our garage sale.

15. Grandma gave Denise a special _____ locket that has been passed down in our family.

16. You have to wash some _____ clothes by hand.

17. I wear sunglasses when the sun is _____ .

18. In order to find out what 4 $\times$ 9 is, I have to _____ .

19. Our new floor lamp will _____ the room.

20. I wrote my name on the _____ line below the date.

Which part of this worksheet was easier to do? Why?

Make a Choice!

Name _____

Choose the correct word to finish each sentence.   Write the words in the blanks.

1. Desert areas are _____ .
                              barren   fertile

2. Water _____ as it freezes.
                    expands   contracts

3. The letter *u* is a _____ .
                                consonant   vowel

4. An angry lion may be _____.
                                    tame   ferocious

5. Kitchens are _____ rooms.
                          interior   exterior

6.   Hospital rooms must be kept _____ .
                                                filthy   clean

7.   A beginning golfer is _____ .
                                  a pro   an amateur

8. Farms are usually in _____ areas.
                                    rural   urban

9. If you miss a school day, you're _____ .
                                                present   absent

10. A mask _____ who you are.
                    conceals   reveals

Fine choices!

Definitions

Knowledge of the semantic features of words is at the very heart of all vocabulary tasks. As a child interacts more and more with her environment, she gathers additional information and knowledge about the semantic features of words. In order to express the definition of a word, she must recognize all the critical semantic attributes of the target word and select those attributes which differentiate the meaning of the target word from words that have similar meanings.

The difficulty of the definitions task is the requirement that the child express the meaning of the word without contextual cues. For example, if a child says the definition of scissors is "a tool for cutting," she has not differentiated scissors from other tools designed for cutting. The physical attributes of a pair of scissors are what make this distinction. A more complete definition of scissors is "two sharp blades which slide past each other to cut something."

The language-delayed child may have difficulty giving complete definitions for target words, possibly due to an underdeveloped vocabulary or an inability to express the words which best describe a concept. These Definitions worksheets help to increase childrens' knowledge of the semantic features of words so that they can clearly differentiate and define words.

Definitions

The Bird Is the Word

Name _____

I'm going to ask you some questions about birds. Color a feather for each correct answer you give.

1.
Do birds have feathers?

2.
What do birds do with their beaks?

3.
Do birds' wings help them chirp?

4.
Do birds roar?

5.
Are birds lighter than airplanes?

6.
Do birds lay eggs?

7.
Do birds eat worms and bugs?

8.
Are all birds blue?

You should be as proud as a peacock!

Clowning Around

Name _____

Clara loves being a clown! Would you like to be one, too? Find out what a clown is and then you can decide. I'll ask you some questions about clowns. For each correct answer you give, color one part of Clara.

1. What do clowns wear?
2. Are all clowns happy? Why?
3. Are all clowns silly? Why?

4. What are some tricks clowns do?
5. Where do clowns work?
6. Are clowns real people? How do you know?

Have you decided to be a clown?

Bear-y Good Words

Name _____

Some of the words on this worksheet tell about bears, and some words don't. I'll help you read the words. Draw a circle around the words that are true about bears. Draw an X through the words that aren't true about bears.

1. Bears have: ears   fur

                     claws   wings

                     antlers   tails

2. Bears can: growl   write

                    drive   chew

                    whistle   run

Bear-y good work!

My New Coat

Name _____

Some children have coats and some have jackets. Let's see how many things you can tell me about coats and jackets. I'll ask you a question, then you can color a part of the coat each time you answer correctly.

1. What do you do with a coat?
2. How do you fasten a coat?
3. When do you wear a coat?

4. Who wears a coat?
5. Why do you wear a coat?
6. Where do you wear a coat?

You got it all buttoned up! Now, finish coloring the rest of the coat!

In the Swim

Do you like to swim? Me, too! Let's see how much you know about swimming by answering these questions. Ready?

When you swim...

1. what do you do with your legs?
2. do you breathe under water? Why not?
3. do you swim alone without an adult watching? Why not?
4. what do you wear?
5. do you dive where it's shallow? Why not?

Let's take a dip!

Way Up High

Some of these pictures are things that are high. Other pictures are things that are not high. Color all the high things blue. Then, tell why each one is high.

1. mountains

2. flower

3. airplane

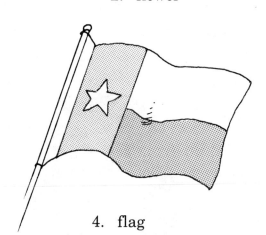

4. flag

5. mitten

6. cloud

Good thinking!

My Best Friend Is...

Name _____

Isn't it nice to have friends? What is a friend? Let's find out what you think a friend is. I'll write down your answers.

Is a friend someone who...

1. makes you laugh?

2. listens to you?

3. gives you hugs?

4. tells you lies?

What does a friend...

1. say when he/she has been mean?

2. do when you call on the phone?

3. give you when you're sad?

4. do when you need help?

That's what friends are for!

Our House Is a Very Fine House

Name _____

Some people live in houses and some live in apartments. Tell about where you live by circling either Yes or No at the end of each sentence. Then, finish the picture to make it look like your home.

My home has _____ .

1. a kitchen	Yes	No
2. a living room	Yes	No
3. a bathroom	Yes	No
4. a basement	Yes	No
5. an attic	Yes	No
6. a garage	Yes	No

We have _____ .

1. neighbors	Yes	No
2. an elevator	Yes	No
3. a fireplace	Yes	No
4. a fire escape	Yes	No
5. stairs	Yes	No
6. a doorbell	Yes	No

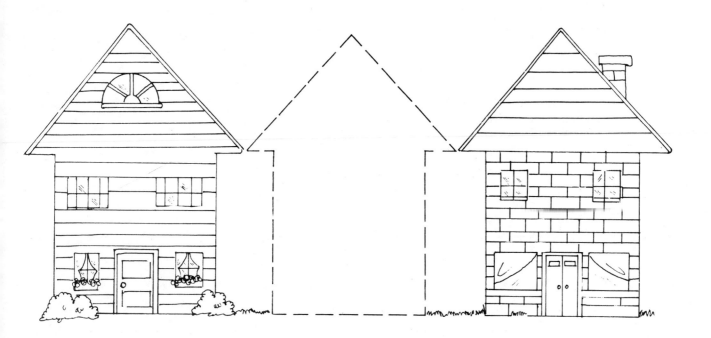

Wherever you live, that's called home.

It's a Mystery!

Read each sentence. Each one will give you a clue about the mystery word. In the space below, draw a picture of the mystery word!

1. I am a toy and a decoration.
2. Most of the time I am round.
3. I am made out of thin rubber.
4. I am small at first, but can get very large.
5. I do not weigh much.
6. I can float in the air.

What am I? Draw a picture of me.

The mystery is solved!

Answer: balloon

Matching Clues

Name _____

Read the clues. Then, draw a line from the clue to the picture it describes. You can do it!

Clues

1. I am an animal's foot.

2. I am an orange vegetable.

3. I help you hear.

4. I am the place where plants grow.

5. I am a tool you use to put nails in wood.

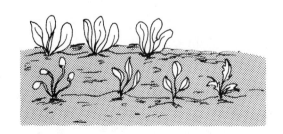

6. I am a very young child.

You matched the clues to the pictures very well!

Happy Birthday!

Read the words in the box. Then, use them to finish the crossword puzzle.

pencil
shoe
sandwich
orange
oven
eagle
lamb
sidewalk

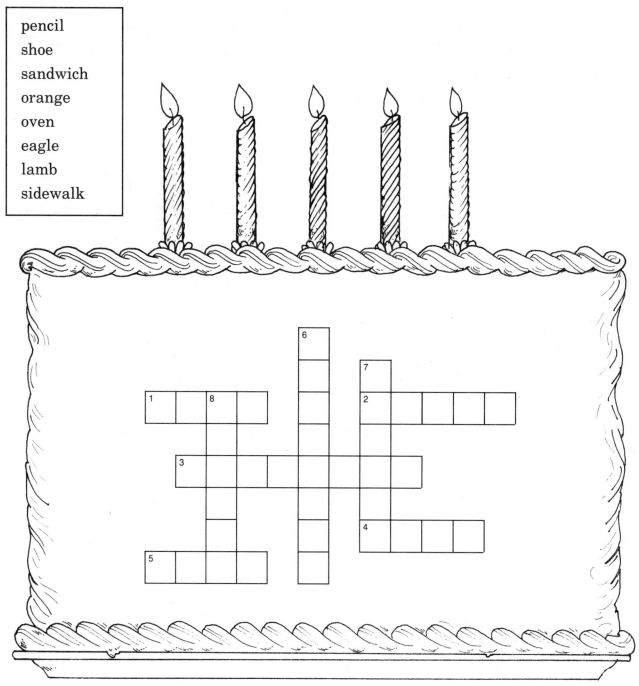

Across

1. wear on your foot
2. U.S. national bird
3. two slices of bread with food between
4. a baby sheep
5. the part of a stove you bake in

Down

6. a safe place to walk
7. you write and erase with this
8. a fruit whose color and name are the same

You deserve a present for your hard work!

Yes or No?

Name _____

Look at each picture. Then, read the questions below it. Circle Yes or No to answer each question.

1. Is a beach by water?   Yes   No

   Is a beach sandy?   Yes   No

   Do you go to the beach in the winter?   Yes   No

   Do we watch a play at the beach?   Yes   No

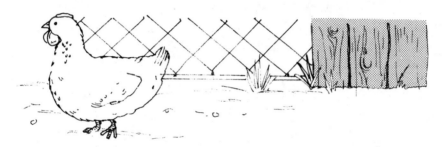

2. Is a chicken a bird?   Yes   No

   Does a chicken live on a farm?   Yes   No

   Can a chicken fly?   Yes   No

   Does a chicken have feathers?   Yes   No

3. Is a raccoon tame?   Yes   No

   Does a raccoon live in the forest?   Yes   No

   Is a raccoon covered with fur?   Yes   No

   Does a raccoon wear a real mask?   Yes   No

Yes! You answered the questions like an expert!

Flower Fun   Name _____

Read each sentence. Then, fill in the blank with a word from the flower. When you're done, color your flower to make it even more beautiful!

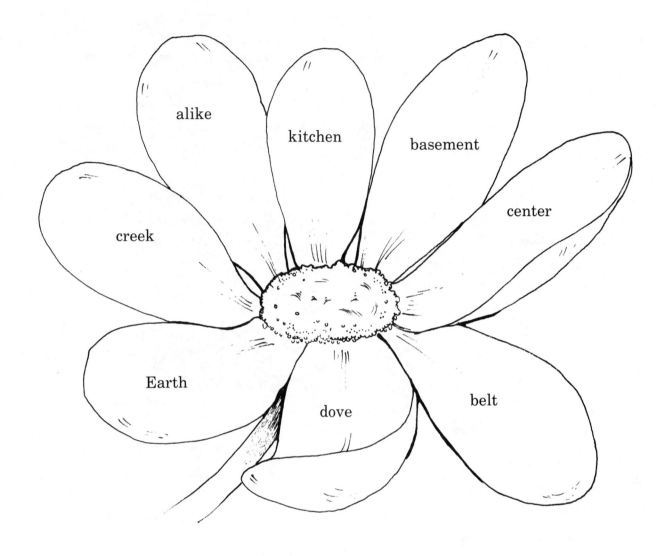

1. When two things are the same, we say they're _____ .

2. Ray tightened his _____ to make sure his pants stayed up.

3. We cook in the _____ .

4. If you're in the middle of something, you're in the _____ .

5. Sandy _____ into the water head first.

6. A _____ is a small stream of water that leads to a river.

7. A room underground is called a _____ .

8. The name of our planet is _____ .

Beautiful!

Round Up

Name _____

Read the word in the box. Then, circle the word below the box that means the same thing. Read each word before you choose your answer!

1.

wonderful

awful

great

simple

sorry

2.

clue

dark

mystery

puzzle

hint

3.

tiny

little

large

trail

narrow

4.

robber

police

thief

jail

mask

5.

pail

carry

cup

bucket

wagon

6.

above

over

under

between

on

7.

often

once

now

late

frequently

8.

toss

spin

pitch

roll

pin

9.

bloom

rose

spring

blossom

leaves

You really know what you're talking about!

You're a Star Student!

Look at each picture. Then, write a word in the blank to describe what's happening in the picture. Use words from the star.

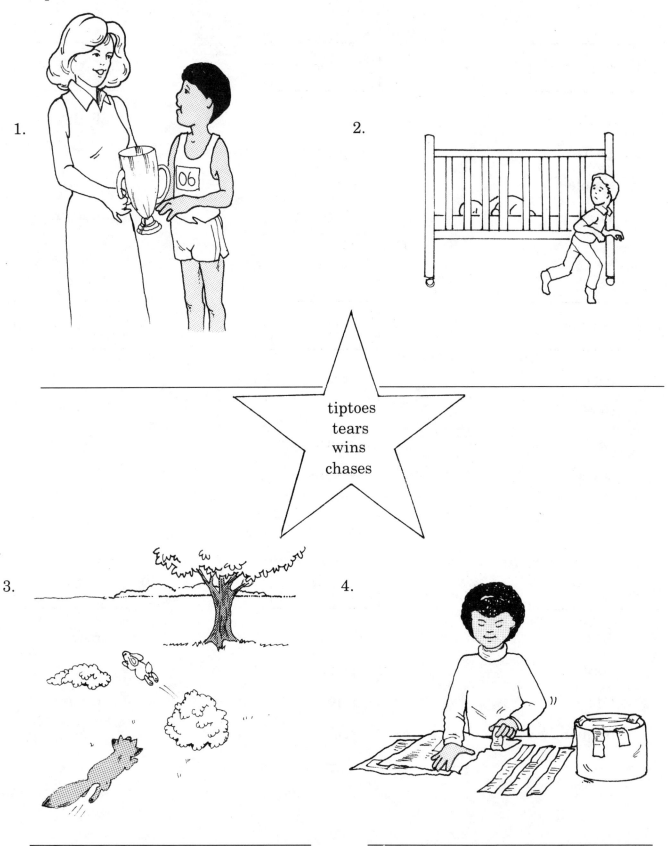

1.

2.

_____

tiptoes
tears
wins
chases

3.

4.

_____   _____

Brilliant!

Can This Be True?

Name _____

Mark an X by each sentence that's true and an O by each sentence that's false. Please read carefully!

1. _____ A brush has bristles.

   _____ You use a brush to fix your hair.

   _____ You wash your hair with a brush.

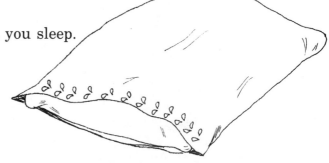

2. _____ You lay your head on a pillow when you sleep.

   _____ A pillow is hard.

   _____ Pillows go on the table.

3. _____ You can sit on a bench.

   _____ A bench is the same as a chair.

   _____ A bench has legs.

4. _____ Many people can ride on a bus.

   _____ A bus is a small vehicle.

   _____ You pay to ride on a city bus.

5. _____ An elevator takes you from one building to another.

   _____ Only one person can ride an elevator at a time.

   _____ You can ride an elevator from floor to floor in a building.

Now, tell why each sentence you marked with an O is false.

Write It Out

Look at each picture. Then, write a sentence to tell what it is. Tell the most important things about each picture.

1.

_____

_____

_____

2.

_____

_____

_____

3.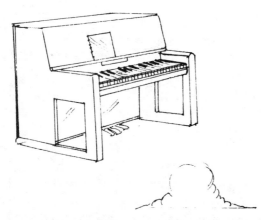

_____

_____

_____

4.

_____

_____

_____

You're right again!

Ready for Riddles?

Read each riddle. Then, write your answer for the riddle in the blank. Try to get each one right!

1. I am food for an animal.
   I grow on a tree.
   I get buried in the fall.
   I am food for a squirrel.
   What am I?   _____

2. I am a mammal.
   I live in Australia or in a zoo.
   I can jump a long distance quickly.
   What am I?   _____

3. We can be dim or bright.
   We shine in the night.
   We are found on the front of a car.
   What are we?   _____

4. I am a reptile.
   I swim in the water or lie in the sun.
   I have a short snout and sharp teeth.
   What am I?   _____

5. I am the upper part of a house.
   I may be used to store things.
   I am right under the roof.
   What am I?   _____

6. I am a piece of cloth.
   I hang in front of a window or a stage.
   I open up when a play starts.
   What am I?   _____

You were ready for these riddles!

DEFINITIONS   193

Puzzle Fun!

Name _____

Fill in this crossword puzzle with the answers to the clues. Get ready for some puzzle fun!

Across

1. a hopping mammal from Australia
2. something unclean in the environment
3. to do something again
4. wing-like part of a fish
5. a payment for regular use of a home

Down

6. engine
7. small nut of an oak tree
8. gray and white bird that lives by the water
9. a bird's nose
10. printed card that allows you to attend a ball game
11. clean and tidy

Fun, wasn't it?!

Match Me

Name _____

Match the words with their definitions. Write the letter of the word in the blank beside its definition.

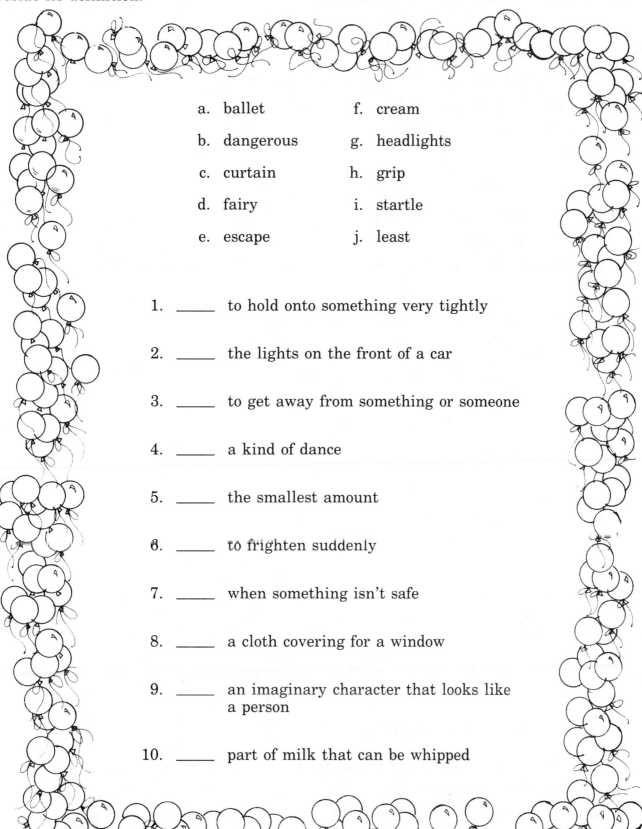

a. ballet   f. cream

b. dangerous   g. headlights

c. curtain   h. grip

d. fairy   i. startle

e. escape   j. least

1. _____ to hold onto something very tightly

2. _____ the lights on the front of a car

3. _____ to get away from something or someone

4. _____ a kind of dance

5. _____ the smallest amount

6. _____ to frighten suddenly

7. _____ when something isn't safe

8. _____ a cloth covering for a window

9. _____ an imaginary character that looks like a person

10. _____ part of milk that can be whipped

Congratulations! You did it!

What Does It Mean?

Name _____

Read each numbered sentence. Then, read the sentences below them. Put an X by the sentence that tells what the numbered sentence means.

1. The boy was ashamed of what he had done.

    _____ He felt guilty because what he did was wrong.
    _____ He felt happy for what he had done.
    _____ He thought he should do the same thing again.

2. The girl took the blame for the broken window.

    _____ She didn't break the window.
    _____ She was responsible for the broken window.
    _____ She didn't know who broke the window.

3. The children were eager for school this morning.

    _____ The children were late for school.
    _____ The children were on time for school.
    _____ The children were anxious for school to start.

4. John and his class went on a hike.

    _____ The students went for a long walk.
    _____ The students went for a bicycle ride.
    _____ The students played on the playground equipment.

5. There was liquid on the floor.

    _____ The floor was covered with carpet.
    _____ The floor had a rug on it.
    _____ The floor had some fluid on it, maybe water or juice.

6. The teacher said, "Don't mumble."

    _____ The teacher meant, "Speak clearly."
    _____ The teacher meant, "Talk louder."
    _____ The teacher meant, "Slow down."

Good answers!

Storytelling Fun

Name _____

Read the story. Then, follow the directions below the story.

My dad and another man own a furniture business. Last Saturday, they sold all kinds of furniture. The people who bought the furniture got it on sale.

After work, my dad and his partner took me to hear a group of people who play musical instruments together. There were many people who also came to hear the group play.

When the man who directs the orchestra walked onto the stage, he fell down. He was wearing a wig and it fell off his head! His face got red and he looked very embarrassed. His face had lots of creases and puckers in it. Saturday was an interesting day for my dad and me!

1. Underline the definition for *audience* with a purple crayon.
2. Underline the definition for *wrinkles* with a black crayon.
3. Underline the definition for *stumbled* with a green crayon.
4. Underline the definition for *bargain* with a red crayon.
5. Underline the definition for *conductor* with an orange crayon.
6. Underline the definition for *orchestra* with a blue crayon.

What's a good name for this story?

Visiting a Museum

Look at the picture below. Then, follow the directions under the picture. Have fun!

1. A visitor is a person who is visiting a place.
    Put an X on each visitor.

2. A passenger is a person who is riding while someone else is driving.
    Put a square around each passenger.

3. A museum is a building where people can see art, science, or history items.
    Color the museum gray.

4. A guard is a person who watches over and protects things or people.
    Circle the guard with a red crayon.

Hope you had a nice visit!

DEFINITIONS   198

Which Is Which?

Name _____

Draw lines to match the words in the right column with the definitions in the left column.

1. A print in a rock of a plant or animal that lived long ago is called a _____ .

    create

2. Beds, dressers, chairs, tables, and couches are pieces of _____ .

    holiday

3. A special day like Christmas or Easter is called a _____ .

    fake

4. To make something new means to _____ .

    fossil

5. When something isn't real, we say it's _____ .

    hive

6. To save someone from danger or from being hurt means to _____ .

    symbol

7. A mark that stands for something else is a _____ .

    furniture

8. The place where bees live is a _____ .

    rescue

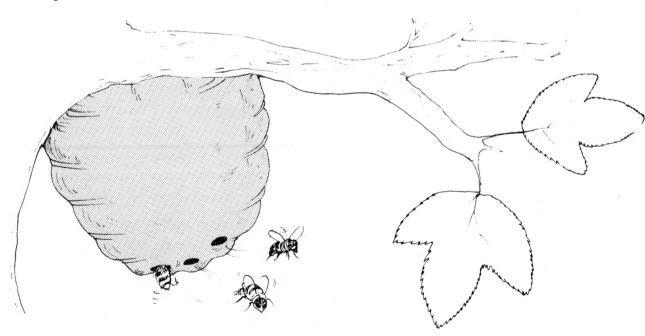

Nice matching!

Sort It Out

Name _____

Read each sentence. Then, circle the best word to finish the sentence.

1. A large sculpture of a person or animal is a _____ .

    portrait   statue   photograph

2. A personal belief about something is an _____ .

    answer   excuse   opinion

3. A person who saw something happen is a _____ .

    witness   follower   leader

4. A medical doctor is also called a _____ .

    musician   physician   physical

5. Someone who competes against you is your _____ .

    ancestor   partner   opponent

6. A person with no courage is a _____ .

    criminal   hero   coward

7. A period of 100 years is called a _____ .

    century   decade   calendar

8. Someone who goes along with you is your _____ .

    competition   companion   campaign

What makes some of these answers hard to choose?

Check It Out!

Name _____

Read each list of clues to describe a word. Then, circle the word that matches each description. These are tricky, so check your work carefully!

1. a kind of weather
    happens in the winter
    has both snow and ice

    thunderstorm   hurricane   blizzard

2. vegetable
    grows in a head
    used to make coleslaw

    lettuce   cabbage   celery

3. male
    entertains
    plays a character

    singer   actress   actor

4. large room
    has many seats in rows
    has a stage

    auditorium   library   cafeteria

5. tool
    long and thin
    used with screws

    hammer   wrench   screwdriver

6. fruit
    red
    tiny seeds on the outside

    cherry   strawberry   apple

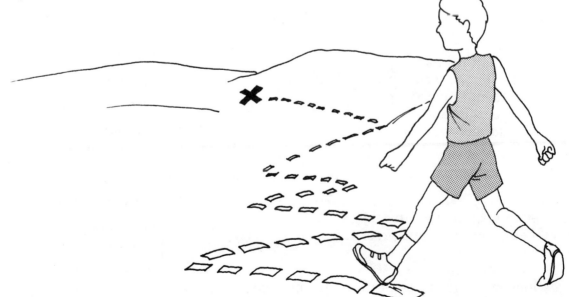

Now, underline the clue that gave you the best information for each riddle. Why do some clues help more than others?

Be a Word Wizard!

Name _____

Use the wizard's clues in the box to help you fill in this crossword puzzle.

Across

1. the taste something has
2. a leg or an arm of a body; a branch of a tree
3. where something comes from
4. a huge rock or stone
5. something old and valuable

Down

1. a cabinet to keep papers in folders
6. a story being told without proof
7. an award
8. a bush or small plant
9. suggestions or criticism given to help someone

boulder

shrub

limb

trophy

rumor

source

advice

antique

file

flavor

You're smart with words!

What Does It Mean?   Name _____

Choose the best word to finish each sentence. Write the word in the blank.

1. If an army moves ahead, that means it _____ .

   retreats   surrenders   advances

2. If you annoy someone, that means you _____ him.

   bother   assist   advise

3. If you admit you did something wrong, that means you _____ .

   agree   confess   pardon

4. If you put two things together, that means you _____ them.

   contain   convince   connect

5. If you compose a song, that means you _____ it.

   write   sing   play

6. If you pause briefly, that means you _____ .

   relax   hesitate   pounce

7. If you watch something, you _____ it.

   observe   magnify   ignore

8. If you set something free, you _____ it.

   endanger   release   capture

Which words were unfamiliar to you? Do you know what they mean now?

Match 'em Up!

Name _____

Match each word to its definition. The first one is done for you.

1. incredible   _____ from many countries

2. accidental   _____ confused

3. eerie   __1__ hard to believe

4. international   _____ dangerous or unhealthy

5. average   _____ spooky or scary

6. harmful   _____ normal

7. excellent   _____ not done on purpose

8. bewildered   _____ of the highest quality

Super matching!

Crazy Riddles!

Name _____

Help! The computer mixed up the clues to these riddles. Write the letter of each clue beside the word it belongs to. The first one is started for you.

WORDS		CLUES
1. gasoline	<u>D</u> ___ ___	A. used for sleeping
		B. mammal
2. hurricane	___ ___ ___	C. made of hair
3. eyebrow	___ ___ ___	D. liquid
		E. a kind of weather
4. dolphin	___ ___ ___	F. on a forehead
		G. lives in an ocean
5. crib	___ ___ ___	H. furniture
		I. made from oil
		J. begins over an ocean
		K. about the size of a shark
		L. above the eyes
		M. used by babies
		N. fuel for cars
		O. has wind and rain

Now, use the three clues for each word to make riddle cards. Write the three clues on an index card for each word. Then, see how many clues your friends need to guess each riddle. Can you think of better clues for these words?

Write the Right Choice

Name _____

Choose a word from the box to finish each definition. Then, write a sentence for each word to show what the word means. The first one is done for you.

competes	argument	tells	brief
answer	wet	guess	scary

1. A glimpse is a _____brief_____ look at something.

   I caught a glimpse of the mayor when we passed his car.

2. An opponent is someone who _____ against you.

   _____

3. A narrator is someone who _____ a story.

   _____

4. A nightmare is a _____ dream.

   _____

5. A solution is an _____ to a problem.

   _____

6. A marsh is a _____ area of land.

   _____

7. A hunch is a _____ about something.

   _____

8. A quarrel is an _____ between people.

   _____

You should be a writer!

Be Descriptive!

Show what the underlined words mean by finishing each sentence. Use the dictionary to find the definitions of words you don't know.

1. A <u>bold</u> person is someone who _____

    _____

2. If something is <u>brief</u>, that means _____

    _____

3. If someone is <u>bald</u>, he _____

    _____

4. A <u>bony</u> animal is an animal that _____

    _____

5. If something is <u>dainty</u>, it _____

    _____

6. A <u>clumsy</u> person is someone who _____

    _____

7. If something is <u>harmless</u>, that means _____

    _____

8. If something is <u>permanent</u>, it _____

How does a dictionary help us?

Could These Be True?

Name _____

Which of these sentences could be true? Circle T for each sentence that could be true and F for each sentence that couldn't be true. Then, think how you can make each false sentence true by changing one word. Write your new sentence below the old one. Go to it!

T   F   1. The huge chandelier in the dining room is very noisy.

_____

T   F   2. We study gases, liquids, and solids in chemistry class.

_____

T   F   3. The frail weightlifter won the championship.

_____

T   F   4. Mother's spaghetti sauce simmered in the freezer.

_____

T   F   5. Nails keep horseshoes on a horse.

_____

T   F   6. Frank is so stingy he never gives tips.

_____

T   F   7. Molly and Ben took the highway to the top of the skyscraper.

_____

T   F   8. Mountain climbing can be treacherous.

_____

You answered truthfully!

Pair These Up

Match the words in the right column with the descriptions in the left column. Be careful. You won't use all the words!

1. _____ a large, vehicle used by a farmer to do field work

2. _____ a contest between several persons or teams

3. _____ to hit at or swing suddenly

4. _____ to depend on someone or something

5. _____ to continue doing something after briefly stopping

6. _____ a special way of doing something

7. _____ a wide-brimmed Mexican hat

8. _____ something used to breathe while swimming under water

a. rely

b. resume

c. tractor

d. sombrero

e. genuine

f. swat

g. scuba

h. arena

i. technique

j. tournament

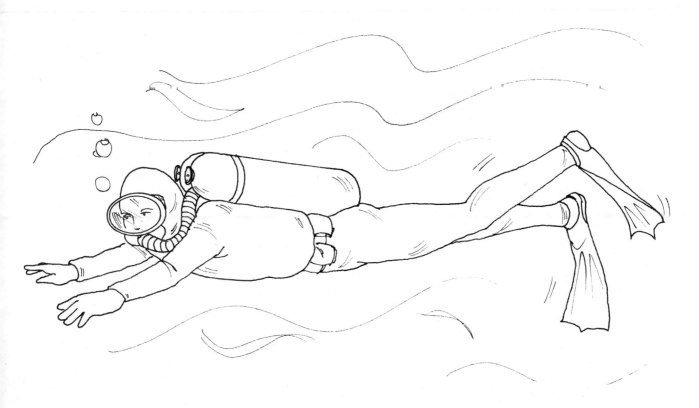

You paired things up very well!

What Does It Mean?

Name _____

Complete the crossword puzzle below using the clues. The first letter of each word is given in the puzzle to help you get started.

Across

1. something that has turned into stone
2. to marry
3. the place where something is
4. to own something
5. chemicals added to soil to make plants grow better
6. a cure for an illness; a solution to a problem
7. suitcases full of clothes

Down

4. a salted snack shaped like a loose knot
5. smoke or gas made when something burns
8. a young deer
9. feeling sleepy
10. the cold area near the North Pole

Truly amazing!

Choose the Best

Name _____

Pick the best word from the box to complete each sentence. Be careful! You won't use all of the words.

tractor	conference	shuttle	bruise
cavern	transistor	hammock	chandelier
plantation	reminder	charcoal	rudder

1. The _____ featured many famous speakers.

2. Lucy had a painful _____ from the accident.

3. The crystal _____ lit up the ballroom.

4. Before she could grill the hamburgers, Linda had to light the _____ .

5. The farmer hitched the plow to his _____ .

6. Cotton was the main crop on the old southern _____ .

7. Mother left a _____ for me to take out the garbage.

8. Rosemary relaxed in the _____ all afternoon.

You chose the very best!

Which of These?

Name _____

Which of these sentences could be true? Circle + for each sentence that could be true and − for each sentence that couldn't be true. Then, think how you can make each false sentence true. Write your new sentence below the old one.

1. + − The lawyer filled her briefcase with work.

   _____

2. + − Monica studied all night for the semester briefcase.

   _____

3. + − The bridge was collided by two strong cables over the canyon.

   _____

4. + − The cab collided with the city bus at the corner.

   _____

5. + − The suspect cooperated with the police investigation.

   _____

6. + − Sally's new pen leaked and the ink cooperated on the paper.

   _____

7. + − The tourists saw the volcano erupt.

   _____

8. + − After landing on the beach, the army erupted the island.

   _____

9. + − Everyone drove their veterinarians through the intersection.

   _____

10. + − The veterinarian placed a splint on the dog's broken leg.

   _____

You get a + for the day!

You Be the Dictionary

Now's your chance to be like a dictionary. Write your best definition for each of the words below. Then, write a sentence using each word. Move over, Webster!

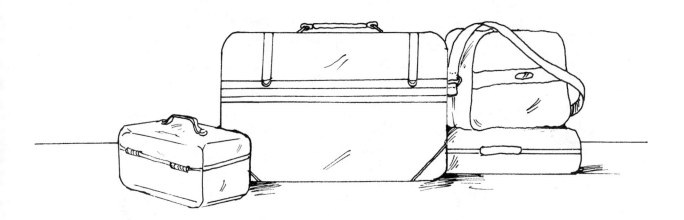

1. luggage: _____

_____

_____

_____

2. tote: _____

_____

_____

_____

3. pedestrian: _____

_____

_____

_____

4. simmer: _____

_____

_____

_____

Excellent definitions!

All in a Day's Work

Name _____

Use words from the horseshoes to complete this story. When you're done, read the story again with all the right words in it.

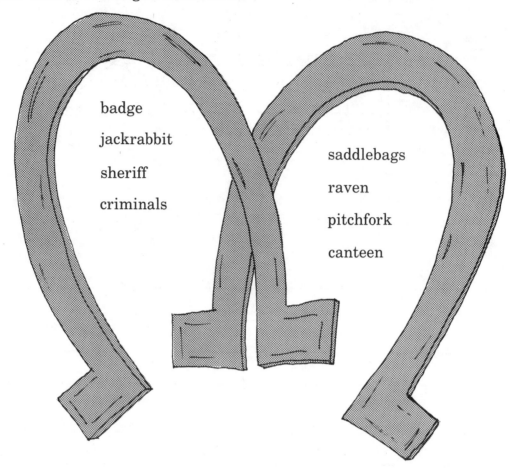

badge

jackrabbit

sheriff

criminals

saddlebags

raven

pitchfork

canteen

Jake Murphy was the _____ of Polk County, Texas. At dawn, he got up,
                                            1.

got dressed, and pinned on his _____ . Jake filled his _____
                                              2.   3.

with supplies and his _____ with water. Down at the barn, he used the
                                    4.

_____ to put fresh straw and hay in the manger for the new horse. He
          5.

saddled his horse and began the ride into town. A _____ hopped away
                                                                        6.

and a _____ flew overhead. As he rode toward town, Jake wondered what
              7.

kind of _____ he would face that day.
                  8.

What's this story about? Tell me in your own words.

Name that Picture

Name _____

Here are four pictures. Write the name of each picture underneath it. Then, think of a sentence using that word and write it in the blanks. Be creative!

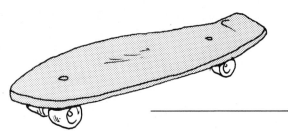

1. _____

   _____

   _____

2. _____

   _____

   _____

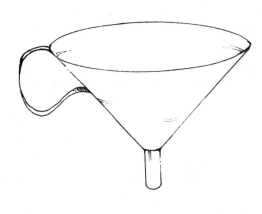

3. _____

   _____

   _____

4. _____

   _____

   _____

Nice writing!

Multiple Definitions

Children learn two types of multiple definition words. The first type includes those words whose definitions are derivatives of the core word. In other words, the key semantic attributes of the core word's definitions also are found in the derivative definitions. For example, two definitions for the word "fly" are "the act of moving through the air" and "an insect." While children must understand the physical properties of "fly" to fully comprehend the meaning, the two definitions do have a common theme or association.

The second type of multiple definition words includes those words in which the multiple definitions do not share a common theme or association. Children learn that a word can have more than one semantically-different meaning and that the multiple definitions have a linguistic core — the word. For example, the two unrelated definitions for the word "duck" are "the act of lowering your head" and "a bird that lives near water." The definitions are learned as separate sets of semantic attributes and the child associates each set with the word. Based on the context of the sentence, the child selects the appropriate meaning to comprehend the complete meaning of the sentence.

Language-delayed children may have difficulty with multiple definitions because of an overall lack of understanding that one word can have several different meanings. These children may be unable to express more than one definition for a word due to word-finding problems or because of significant deficits in usable vocabulary. These Multiple Definitions worksheets are designed to help language-delayed children understand the two types of multiple definition words and to learn how to express meanings in context.

Multiple Definitions

Pick a Pair of Friends

Name _____

Look at these picture pairs. Each pair sounds the same, right? Right, but they mean different things! Tell about each picture. Then, cut out the shapes and give each one to a friend. See if each friend can find his picture pair match!

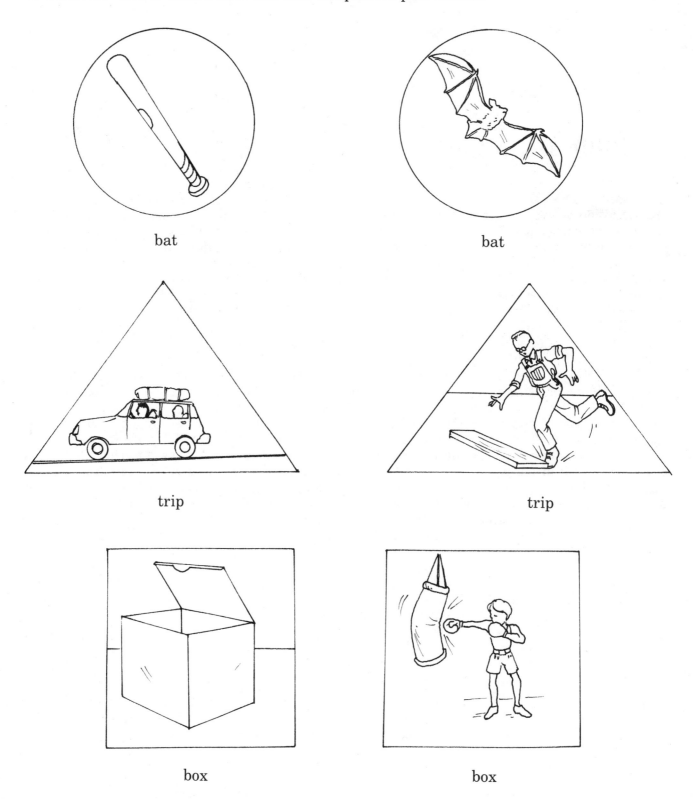

bat   bat

trip   trip

box   box

Did your picture pair friends find each other? What a match-maker!

Seeing Double

Look very carefully! Can you find picture pairs that sound the same but have different meanings? You can? Great! Let's get going!

1. Find two pictures of glasses. Draw a blue line under them.

2. Do you see the two pictures of star? Color them yellow.

3. I see two pictures of top. Do you? Color them green.

4. Look carefully to find two pictures of tire. Draw an orange circle around them.

5. Here's a tricky one. Find two pictures of draw. Color them black.

No double trouble for you!

Join the Band

Look at this silly band! Now, listen carefully. Color the pictures of feet red. Draw a blue line under each picture of a bat. Then, draw a green X on the two pictures of top.

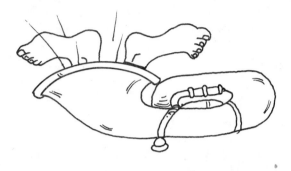
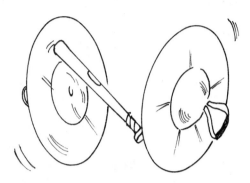

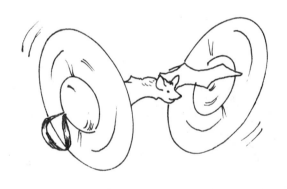

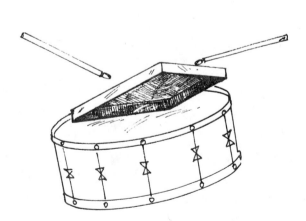
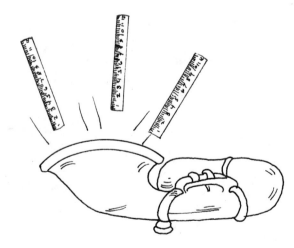

What beautiful music you make!

Apples Galore

Name _____

Listen to the message on each apple. Color the two apples with the word *right* on them red. Color the two apples with the word *kind* on them yellow. Finally, color the two apples with the word *light* on them green.

Which kind of apple do you like best?

Birthday Boxes

It's Douglas Dinosaur's birthday! He opened his presents, but he's having trouble matching them up. Cut out the pictures at the bottom and put them in the right box at the top.

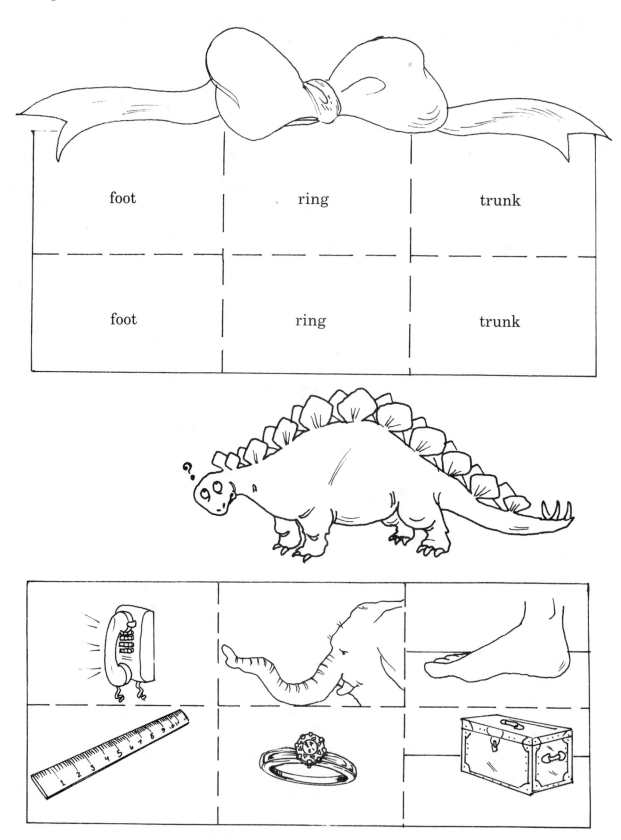

foot	ring	trunk
foot	ring	trunk

Hope your next birthday is happy, too!

Mixed Up Match Up

Help! This page is all mixed up. Find a picture in column Y that sounds exactly the same as a picture in column Z. Draw a line to connect them.

Y   Z

fall

back

cook

Great line up! Now, think of a rhyming word for each picture pair.

Nuts to You

Squire Squirrel is getting ready for winter. Help him gather acorns. Cut them out and put them together if they sound alike. Don't be fooled! Squire Squirrel knows the words may sound alike, but they don't mean the same thing.

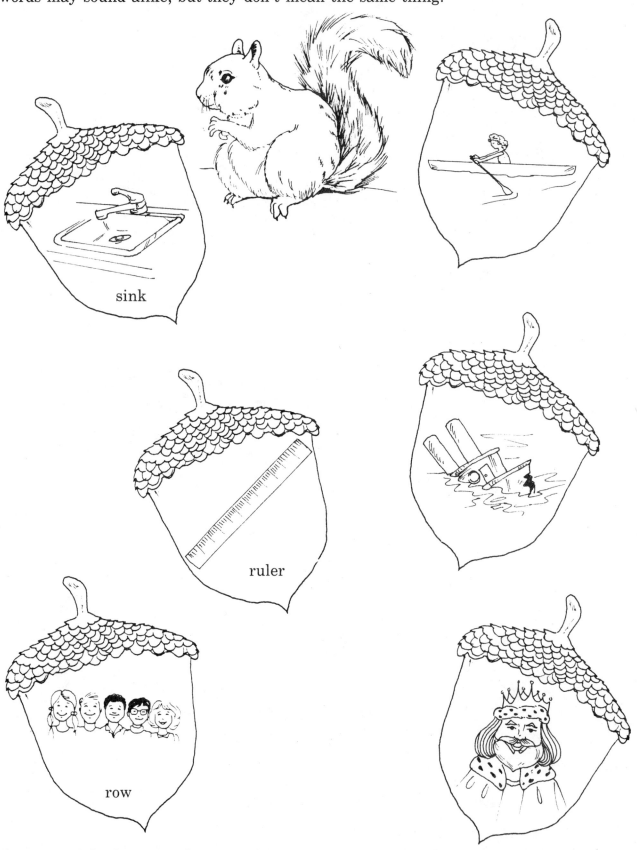

sink

ruler

row

Are you ready for winter?

Big Wheel

Cut out the pictures and glue them on their matching words. Then, tell about each picture pair.

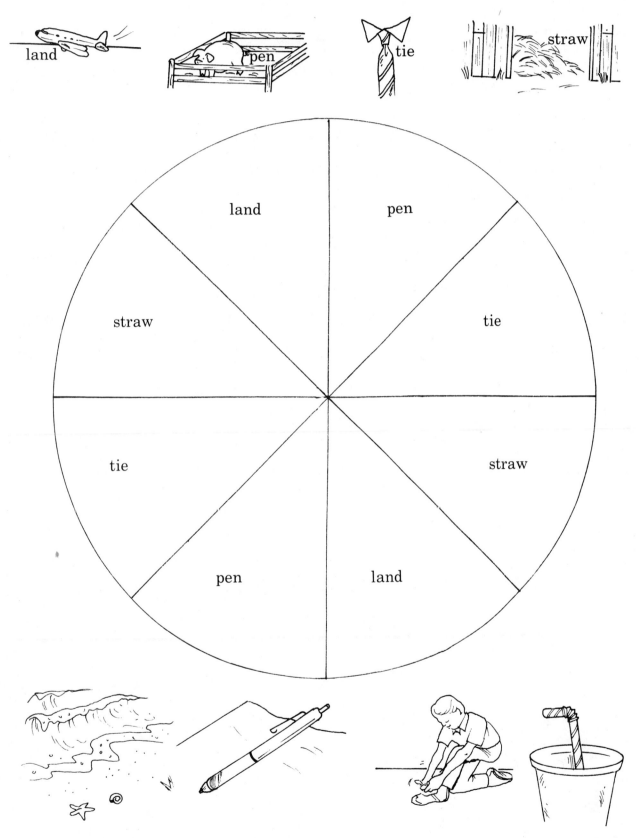

land

pen

tie

straw

You rolled right along!

Steel's Hardware Store

Name _____

Steel's Hardware Store is very busy! Can you help by finding the word pairs that sound the same but mean different things? Thanks!

Find two pictures of the word *sign*. Draw a circle around both of them.
Find two pictures of the word *paint*. Draw an X on both of them.
Find two pictures of the word *feed*. Draw a happy face on both of them.

Thanks! You were a helpful hardware person!

Hare Today, Gone Tomorrow

Name _____

Harry Rabbit has grown a wonderful vegetable garden. Pick the pictures on the vegetables that sound alike, but mean different things. Go ahead! Cut the veggies out and match up the words that sound alike! Then, tell about them.

March

march

nut

nut

bowl

bowl

Now you can munch on your matches!

Let It Snow

Let's make a snowflake! Draw a line between the two words that sound the same.
Tell how each word is different. When you're all done, you'll have a big snowflake!

watch

miss   steps   stick

What a pretty snowflake!

Super Shopper

The Word Store is having a sale. You can buy two words for the price of one! Find the price tags that match. Draw different colored circles around each pair of price tags. Then, write the names of the pictures on the lines below them. The pictures with the same prices should have the same names. If you match all the picture pairs, you'll be a Super Word Shopper!

1.

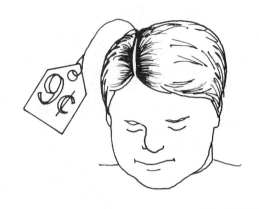

_____

2.

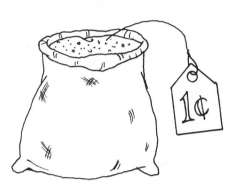

_____

3.

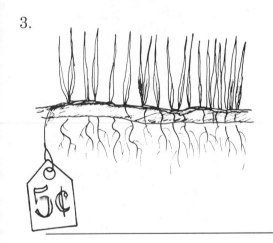

_____

4.

_____

5.

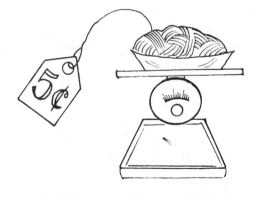

_____

6.

_____

You just earned 15¢ for your bank!

MULTIPLE DEFINITIONS   229

To My Sweetheart

Name _____

Here are some pretty hearts for next Valentine's Day. Draw a pretty colored ribbon between the two words that sound the same but have different meanings.

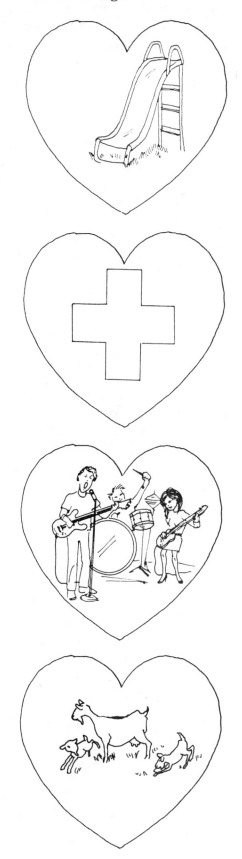

band

slide

kids

cross

Your heart was really in this project!

Who Sees What?

Name _____

Sue and Sandra are best friends, but they don't always think the same. Sometimes, when they hear a word, they picture different things in their minds. Look at the pictures in their minds and tell how they are different.

1.

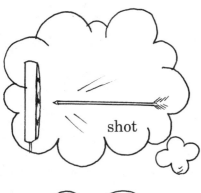

2.

3.

Isn't our mind's eye amazing?

School Days, School Days

Name _____

Cut out the pictures below. Match them to their places on this old school. Tell about each picture. Then, color the school red.

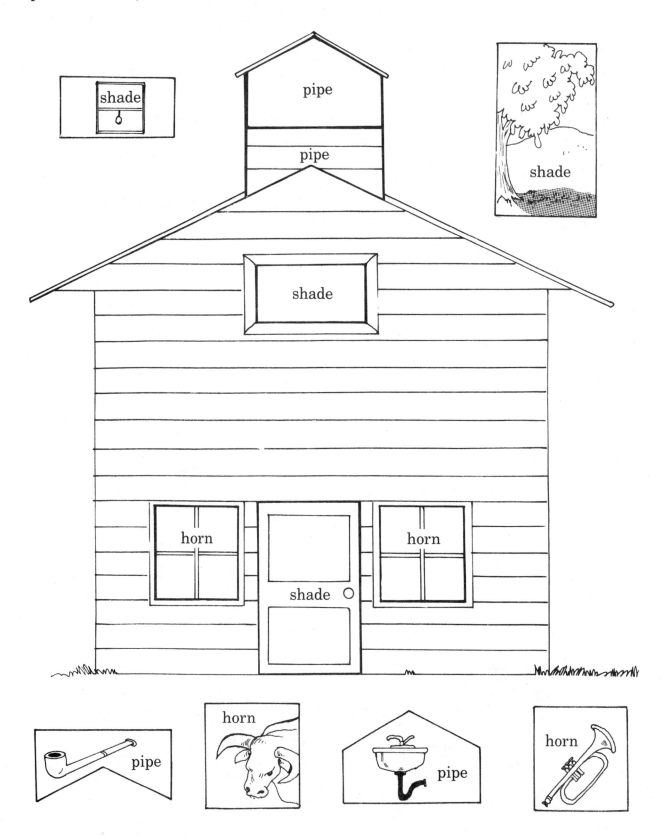

Would you like to go to a one-room school like this?

Snow Fort Fun

Name _____

Isabelle lives in an igloo and goes to school in one, too. After school, she plays in the snow. Help Isabelle build this snow fort. Cut out the ice blocks at the bottom of this page and tell about each one. Then, glue them in their spaces to make a snow fort!

Snow fun is c-c-cold fun!

Dandy Designs

Name _____

Cut these squares apart and match the designs. Do you see a word inside each design?
Good! Each word has two meanings. Talk about the two meanings for each word.
Then, glue your dandy designs together.

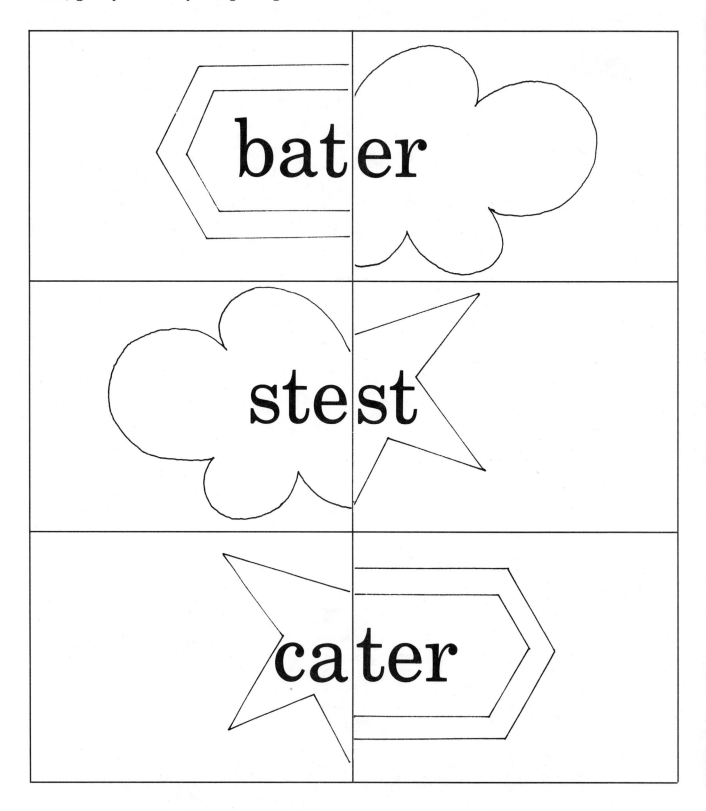

You made beautiful designs out of this mess! That's dandy!

Climbing the Walls

Name _____

Each pair of footprints has the same word written on it. Tell two meanings for each word. Then, cut out the footprints and tape them on a wall!

1.

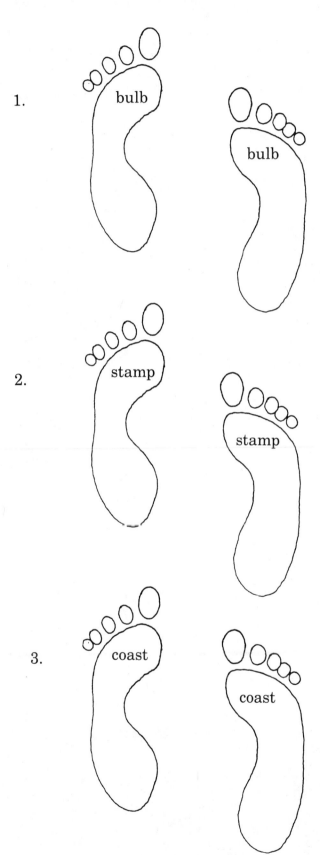

bulb

bulb

2.

stamp

stamp

3.

coast

coast

What smart feet you have! Are they ticklish, too?

Pots o' Words

Name _____

Here's your chance to plant some beautiful flowers! Cut out the flowers and plant two in each pot by matching the words to the pictures. Tell about each flower word pair.

hood

palm

pitcher

Did you give some flowers to somebody special?

Title Two-somes!

Name —————

Summer means lots of time for reading. Pretend you're checking these books out from the library. Explain the title of each book pair. Then, guess what each book is about.

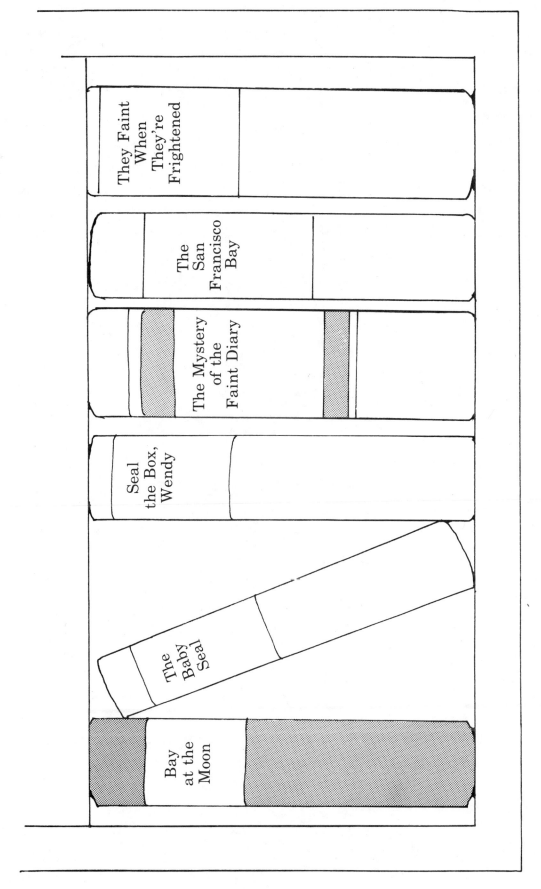

They Faint When They're Frightened

The San Francisco Bay

The Mystery of the Faint Diary

Seal the Box, Wendy

The Baby Seal

Bay at the Moon

Which title is the most exciting? Would you like to write a book someday?

Charlotte's Web

Name _____

Help Charlotte weave her web. Use each word in a sentence to tell what it means.
Each word is in the web two times, so you need to think of two different meanings for
the same word. Start with the number 1. Draw a line connecting the words in order
as you finish each sentence. When you're done, Charlotte will have her new web!

beam
1.

film
3.

record
6.

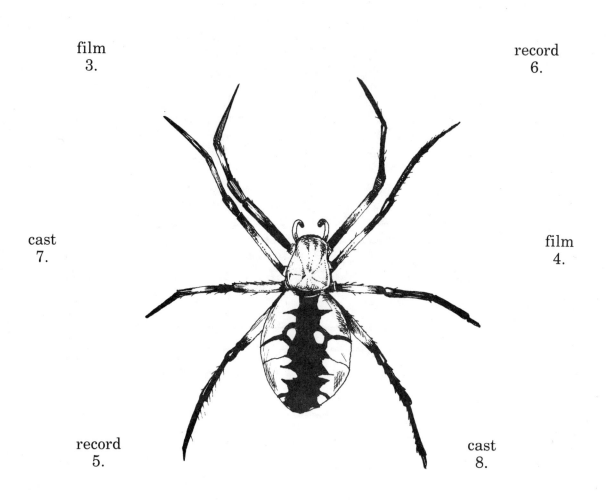

cast
7.

film
4.

record
5.

cast
8.

beam
2.

What a tangled web you weave!

The Great Frame-Up

Name _____

Match the words in the center of the frame with the pictures on the outside of the frame. You'll find two pictures for each word. Draw a line from the pictures to the word. Then, tell the two meanings for each word.

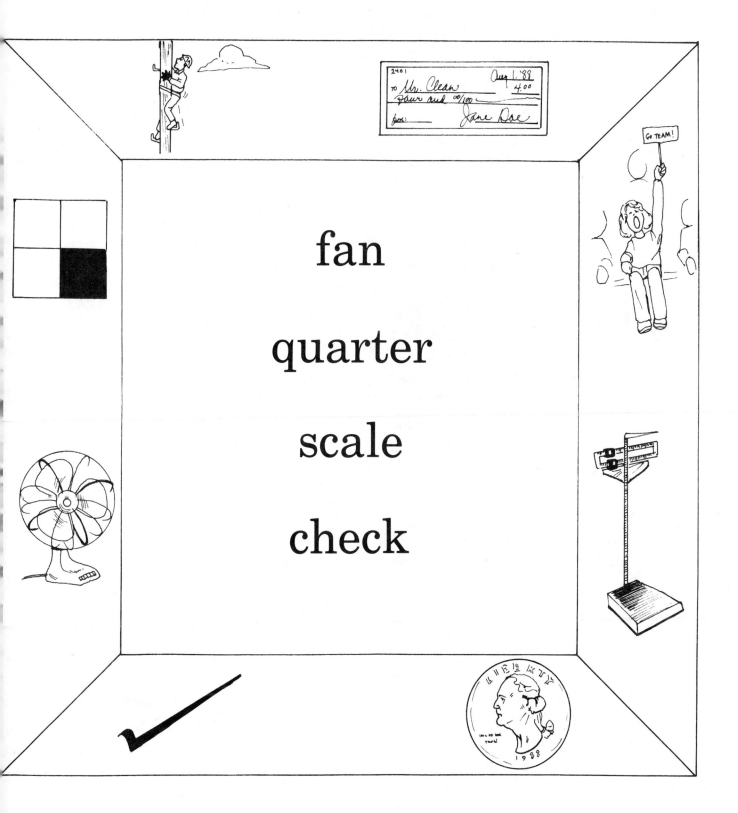

fan

quarter

scale

check

Good work! There's no "framing" you!

Flag Day

Cut out each flag. Hang two flags on each pole by matching the pictures with the words. Describe each picture. Then, color each flag any color you'd like.

buck   picket   sole

What a banner day for your work!

Photographer's Nightmare

Name _____

Phil doesn't know which pictures go together. Draw lines to match the pictures that sound the same. Then, write the word below each picture and tell what it means. Thanks!

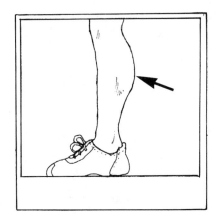  

1. _____   2. _____

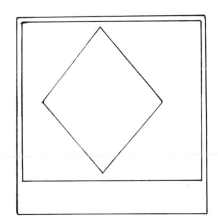 

3. _____   4. _____

 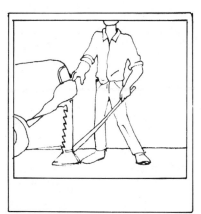

5. _____   6. _____

You finished in a snap! Phil says, "Whew!"

Alien Alert!

Name _____

These aliens don't understand our language. Tell two meanings for each word. Then, cut out each planet and string thread through each one. Hang the planets from your ceiling to make your own galaxy!

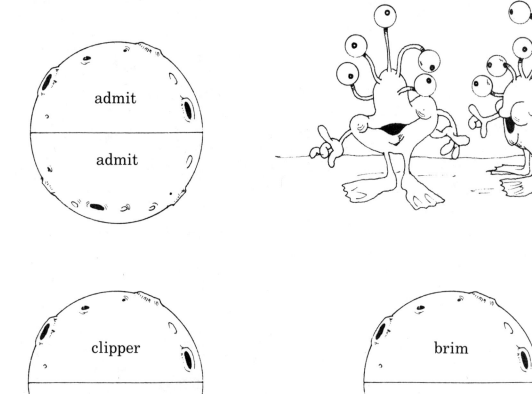

admit

admit

clipper

clipper

brim

brim

date

date

limb

limb

Your work is out of this world!

Wheeler Dealer

Name _____

Tell the meaning of each word in the word pairs. Then, draw a circle around each word to give these dirt bikes some wheels. Draw a flag on the back of each bike for safety.

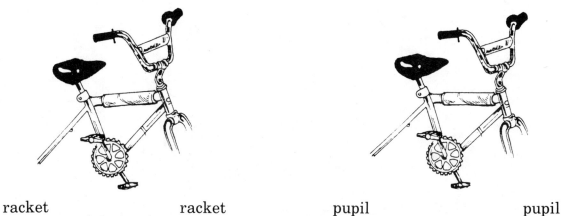

racket   racket   pupil   pupil

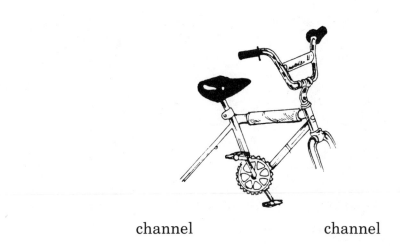

channel   channel

bluff   bluff   dough   dough

Can you do wheelies on your bike?

Prehistoric Picture Match

Name _____

Each of these dinosaurs lives in a cave. Draw a line from each dinosaur to his cave by matching the words. Then, use each word in a sentence to tell what it means.

Now, tell what prehistoric means.

Computer Mania

Name _____

Match each disk to the correct computer monitor. Draw a line to connect each of the word pairs that are the same. Then, use each word in a sentence to tell what the word means. Each word has two meanings, so give two good sentences!

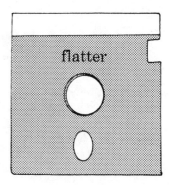

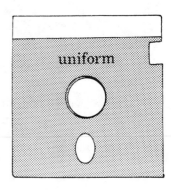

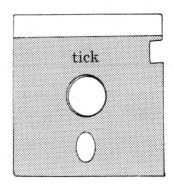

Press any key to continue!

The WORD Award

Name _____

Congratulations! You've won the award for having the best vocabulary in the class. Show how good you are by using each underlined word in a sentence. A clue is given with each word to get you started.

a river <u>barge</u>

<u>barge</u> into a room

a roller <u>coaster</u>

use a <u>coaster</u>

a <u>bun</u> hairdo

a hamburger <u>bun</u>

Congratulations! Those were award-winning sentences!

The WORD Search

Name _____

There are five words in this word search. See if you can find them by searching across, up and down, and diagonally. Draw a line around each word you find. Then, tell two definitions for each. Remember, each word will have two meanings!

HAIL   TISSUE   OUTLET   PELT   DRAFT

B	L	Q	U	O	V	Y	U	D
T	I	S	S	U	E	M	I	D
S	A	R	F	T	O	Z	R	P
W	H	P	E	L	T	A	Y	B
X	G	C	Z	E	F	H	J	K
J	M	O	N	T	I	S	U	E

Excellent searching! You should be an explorer!

Multiple Meaning Crossword

Name _____

This crossword puzzle is special. It uses each word twice by giving two definitions for each word. After writing each word in the puzzle, use it in a sentence.

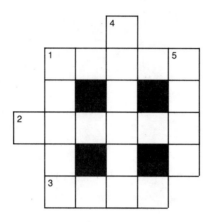

ACROSS

1. what men are called in England
2. a person who sleeps in a tent
3. another name for the ocean or sea

DOWN

1. what cowboys wear over their jeans when they ride horses
4. a recreational vehicle
5. the sport Californians love to do

No cross words about this puzzle . . . it was fun!

A Better Idea

Name _____

You know your ideas are good, so here's a chance to show them! Use the underlined words in each light bulb in two different sentences. There are clues with the words to help you get started.

1.
brand
of soup

brand
a cow

2.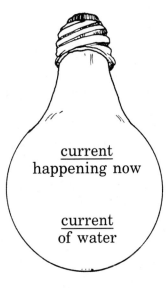
current
happening now

current
of water

3.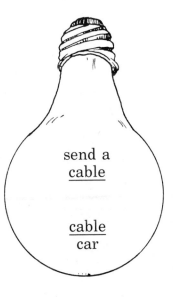
send a
cable

cable
car

4.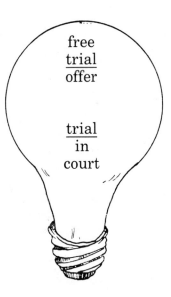
free
trial
offer

trial
in
court

What bright ideas you have!

Directory Assistance

Name _____

Here's an unusual way to practice multiple meanings for words. Dial your phone number. For each number you dial, use the word on the button in a sentence that tells the word's meaning. If you get the same word twice, use the word in different sentences to show that the word has two meanings. After using your phone number, try your best friend's number, too!

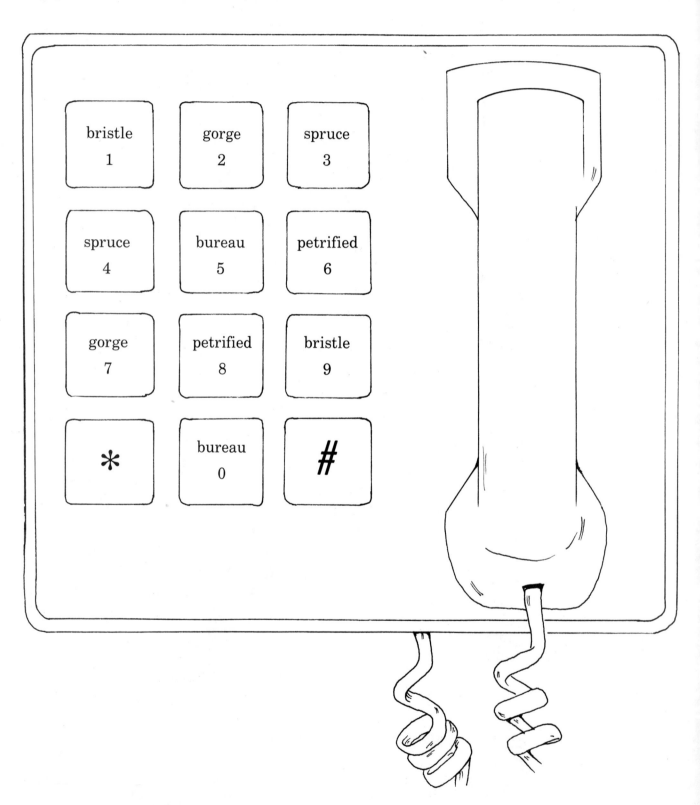

What a word operator you are!

Let's Play Basketball

Name _____

It's basketball season and you're the high scorer on the team. Draw a circle around each of these letters you find in the puzzle: A, C, E, F, L, M, N, O, R, S, T, U, W.

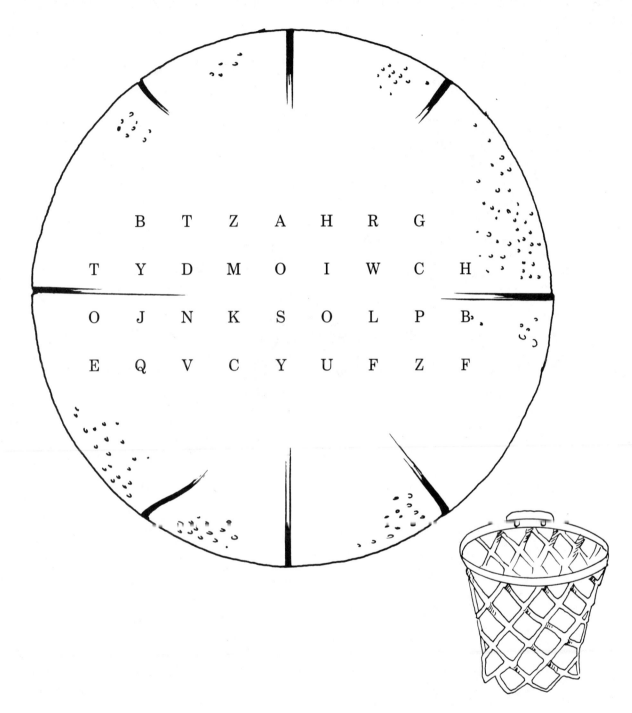

```
        B   T   Z   A   H   R   G
    T   Y   D   M   O   I   W   C   H
    O   J   N   K   S   O   L   P   B
    E   Q   V   C   Y   U   F   Z   F
```

Now, put the circled letters in these blanks, starting with the first letter, *T*. Give two free-throw sentences for each word and you'll lead your team to victory!

___ ___ ___ ___   ___ ___ ___   ___ ___ ___ ___   ___ ___ ___ ___

No fouls along the way? Great!

Skateboard Sanchez

Name _____

Tony Sanchez is the skateboard champ of Wilson Junior High, but he needs your help. He can't think of multiple meanings for words like you can. Tell a meaning for each skateboard word to help Tony improve his vocabulary. Helping someone is a good way to make a new friend!

1.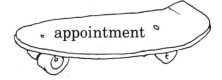

2.

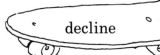

3.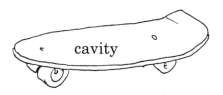

4.

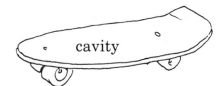

Thanks for helping Tony. He'll roll right through his vocabulary now!

Double Strength

Name _____

Wong Lee is a body builder and an excellent student. He doesn't know English very well yet because he just moved to the U.S. last year. Help Wong understand that some words in our language have more than one meaning. Tell Wong two meanings for each word.

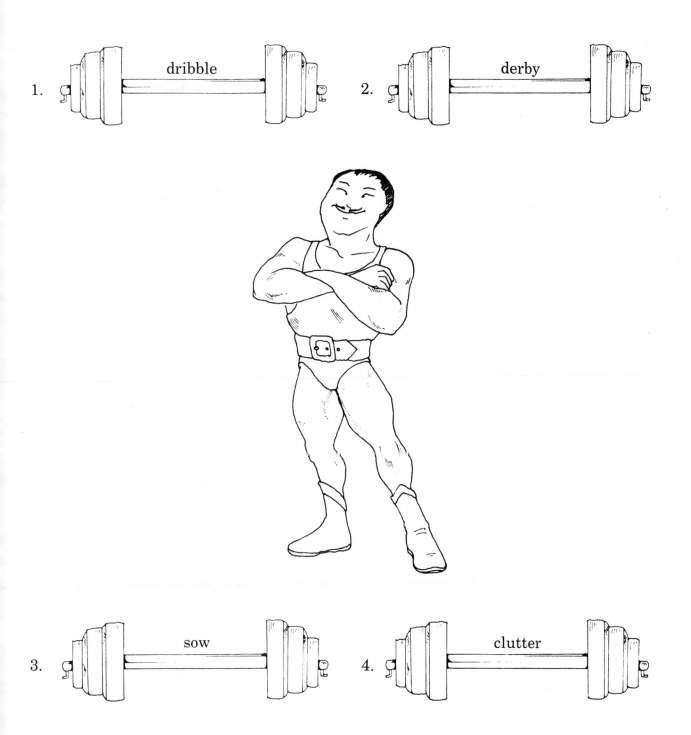

1. dribble

2. derby

3. sow

4. clutter

Thanks! New students always appreciate extra help!

Postcard Homework

Name _____

Gil and Robert are cousins who live in different states. They like to test each other to see who's smarter. These are sentence starters for multiple meaning words they sent to each other. See if you can finish the sentences. Robert and Gil couldn't!

---

1. Clint hit a <u>foul</u>...

2. The lawyer <u>grilled</u> his client...

3. We caught <u>pike</u>...

4. Lisa ran toward the <u>vault</u>...

5. I'll have to <u>decline</u> your offer...

Robert Washington
4150 11th Street
Elseville, IL
09240

---

6. The <u>foul</u> smell...

7. The barbecue <u>grill</u>...

8. The toll on the <u>pike</u>...

9. The bank <u>vault</u>...

10. The <u>decline</u> down the mountain...

Gil Hanover
108 Gerber, Apt. 5
Waynetown, OH
43952

You make a super word star!

Sign Up

Name _____

Follow the signs to word success. Give two meanings for each word. Then, see if you can tell what the signs really mean by their shapes. Watch out! These are hard!

1. 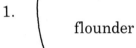 flounder

2. fuse

3. draft

4. 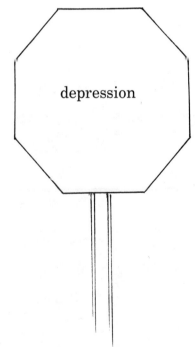 depression

5. yield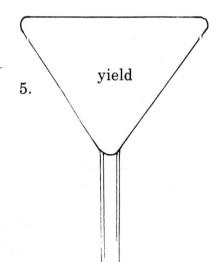

I'll bet you guessed two shapes right!

Cinco de Mayo

May 5th is a day of celebration in Mexico. Support the fiesta by helping the Mariachi band finish their homework, put on their sombreros, and get to the party! Maybe they'll let you play the maracas after you give two sentences for each word!

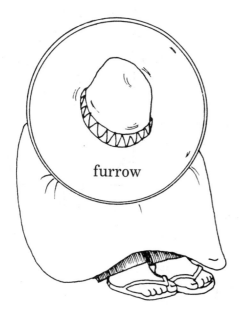

furrow

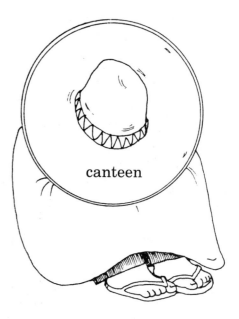

canteen

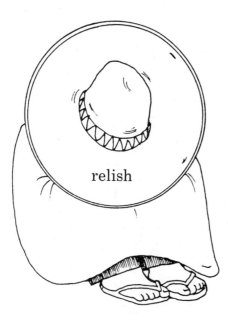

relish

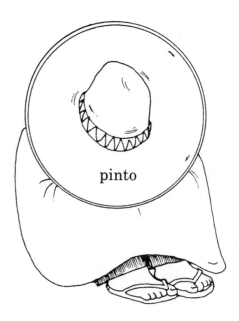

pinto

Gracias!

Bubble Trouble

No gum chewing allowed in school, right? Well, the whole baseball team got caught chewing gum in the gym. Now, they have to do extra multiple meaning words before practice. Can you help them out by telling two definitions for each word in a bubble?

1.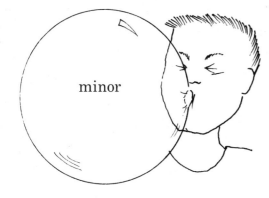

2.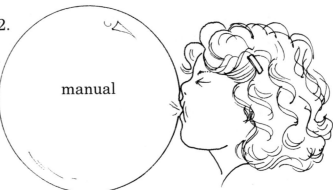

3.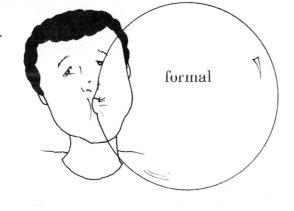

4.

Thanks, sport!

ANSWER KEY

Associations

I'm Seeing Red!, page 8

1, 2, 3, 7, 8

Furniture Sale!, page 9

1, 3, 5, 6

Shape Up, page 11

1. circle
2. rectangle
3. triangle

See the Light, page 12

1, 3, 5, 6

Just Like Another, page 13

1. car, tricycle — things to ride
2. ice cream, pie — desserts
3. nickel, dime — coins
4. canoe, ship — boats

Animal Match, page 14

1 and 6   7. farm
3 and 2   8. young
5 and 4   9. older

Some Like It Hot, page 15

hot: 1, 4, 5
cold: 2, 3, 6

How Are They Alike?, page 16

1. skateboard, bicycle — things to ride
2. flower, tree — things that grow
3. umbrella, rain boots — things to use in the rain
4. sock, sandal — things to wear on your feet

Color Me True, page 17

1. hairbrush, comb, hair pick — things used to comb hair
2. revolving door, gate, door — things you open or close to enter or leave a place
3. ruler, yardstick, tape measure — things used to measure
4. shirt, dress, shorts — clothing

Pack Your Bags, page 18

1. socks, blouse, jacket
2. pretzels, apple
3. comic book, book

These Don't Belong!, page 20

1. flower — not a body of water
2. sack — not used as luggage
3. letter M — not a number
4. soda pop — not a snack to eat

Light or Heavy?, page 21

light — fly, sack, feather, bee
heavy — man, pig, house, bed

Oceans of Fun, page 22

3, 5, 6, 7, 8

Desert Treasure, page 23

TV, iron — Electrical appliances would not work in the desert without electricity.

Where on Earth?, page 24

Across
1. playground
2. bedroom
3. kitchen
4. hospital

Down
2. beach
5. garden
6. ocean
7. circus
8. farm

Feeling Great!, page 25

1. sharp   4. soft
2. soft   5. sharp
3. rough   6. soft

Mixed-Up Map, page 26

telephone, bathtub, alligator, police officer — They are not locations.

Riddle Ravel, page 27

1. horse   4. puzzle
2. owl   5. pig
3. ball   6. pillow

Leo the Lion, page 28

1. leaves, trunk, branches
2. paws, barking, puppies
3. feathers, wings, beak
4. gallop, neigh, hooves

All Together Now, page 30

1. small child — located up in the air
2. skateboard — have wings to fly
3. necktie — furniture

Strong Connections, page 31

People   stranger
             grandfather
             wife
             adult
             uncle
Places   hospital
             meadow
             village
             garden
             island

Things   book
             blanket
             penny
             wagon
             mirror

Yum, Yum!, page 32

1. C   8. D
2. A   9. B
3. D   10. D
4. A   11. C
5. C   12. A
6. A   13. C
7. B   14. B

Calling All Categories!, page 33

Across
1. birds
2. meals
3. emotions
4. sports

Down
1. berries
5. weapons
6. planets
7. crooks
8. grain

Out of Place, page 34

1. c — not a preposition
2. d — not a meal
3. a — not something you sit on
4. b — not a flower
5. c — not something you read
6. a — not baseball player position
7. d — not a size
8. c — not located in kitchen
9. b — not a month
10. d — not jewelry
11. a — not a toy
12. c — not cold
13. c — not a tool
14. b — not a texture
15. a — not something to write with

A Colorful Day, page 35

They are colors.

Planting Time, page 36

1. B   11. C
2. C   12. D
3. A   13. C
4. B   14. B
5. D   15. A
6. B   16. C
7. C   17. C
8. A   18. B
9. D   19. A
10. B   20. C

Everything in Common, page 37

1. They work at a school.
2. They are units of measure.
3. They are large bodies of water.
4. They are jewelry.
5. They are different kinds of shoes.

Pioneer Days, page 38

Things that don't belong: cars, electricity, telephone, skateboard, skyscraper, radio — These are modern inventions.

Be a Good Sport, page 39

1. C   11. A
2. A   12. C
3. B   13. B
4. A   14. A
5. B   15. A
6. C   16. C
7. A   17. A
8. B   18. C
9. B   19. B
10. C   20. C

Home at Last, page 40

1. A   11. A
2. A   12. B
3. D   13. C
4. B   14. A
5. D   15. E
6. C   16. C
7. A   17. D
8. D   18. B
9. C   19. A
10. E   20. B

Make a Choice!, page 41

1. metals   5. fuels
2. weapons   6. building
3. tastes   7. insects
4. window   8. mail

Solid or Liquid?, page 42

1. S   13. S
2. S   14. L
3. L   15. S
4. S   16. S
5. S   17. L
6. L   18. S
7. L   19. S
8. S   20. L
9. S   21. S
10. S   22. S
11. S   23. L
12. L   24. L

Everything's Coming Up Roses!, page 43

instrument — flute, piano, trombone, violin
vegetable — onion, peas, lettuce, corn
toy or game — doll, skates, baseball, football
emotion — anger, joy, pride, greed

It's Your Choice, page 45

1. body parts
2. occupations
3. wild animals
4. clothes

259

Copyright © 1988 LinguiSystems, Inc.

Associations

Vocabulary Quiz, page 46

1. physician, medicine, surgeon — Recreation is not related to medical things.
2. love, honor, cherish — Despise is not a positive feeling.
3. gossip, converse, discuss — Stare is not a type of conversation.
4. drizzle, raindrop, showers — Icicle is not related to rainfall.
5. century, year, months — Second is not a measure of days or years.

Closely Linked, page 47

1. banister — They are things you ride.
2. comrade — They are occupations.
3. dark — They are colors.
4. potato — They are fruits.

Synonyms

Say It Again!, page 50

1. The rabbit jumped into the sack.
2. Andrew picked up a small stone.

Change Up!, page 51

1. The kids saw the pretty lady.
2. Father washes the automobile each Saturday.

Say These Two Ways!, page 52

1. The cheerful chef made some lemonade.
2. The little lad on the ship is wearing a coat and a hat.

Tell Me Again!, page 53

sea, ocean
rabbit, bunny, hare
kids, children
hat, cap
boat, ship

In Your Own Words, page 54

coat, hat, mom, shop, kids, hat, coat, bag, picture, smiles

Think of a Different Way, page 55

1. The cops searched for the robber in the woods.
2. Grandfather hammered nails in the basement.

How Sharp Are You?, page 56

father, dad
plane, jet
beach, shore
sea, ocean
sack, bag
pail, bucket
bathing suit, swimming suit

Help Tell a Story!, page 57

mom, note, mug, plates, sack, road

Face Up to It!, page 58

1. angry   3. unhappy
2. happy

Twice As Nice, page 59

1. present, gift
2. soil, dirt
3. tear, rip
4. throw, toss

Double Duty, page 60

1. dishes   3. beach
2. ill   4. trail

Are You on the Ball?, page 61

1. behind, back
2. over, above
3. between, middle
4. beside, next

Double Trouble, page 62

1. engine, motor
2. car, auto
3. shack, hut
4. pole, post
5. highway, road, street

Missing Vowels, page 63

1. blossom, bloom
2. wise, smart
3. large, huge
4. frighten, scare
5. paste, glue
6. twirl, spin
7. finished, done

Name It Again, page 64

1. champion, winner
2. trumpet, cornet
3. spine, backbone
4. creek, stream

Describe This!, page 65

1. A photo and a present are on the dresser. A picture and a gift are on the chest.
2. There are pants on the chair. There are slacks on the chair.

Make Your Choice, page 66

1. timid   4. author
2. hare   5. demand
3. silent   6. trash

Puzzling Word Puzzles, page 67

1. over   6. under
2. rock   7. pretty
3. yell   8. save
4. mix   9. kids
5. simple

Match 'em Up, page 68

1. grin   5. lid
2. mistake   6. spoiled
3. frightened 7. wound
4. joyful   8. strange

Triple Trouble, page 69

1. dawn
2. bewildered
3. chose
4. commercial
5. porpoise

Double Letters, page 70

1. creek   6. terrible
2. common   7. ill
3. fall   8. accident
4. dresser   9. college
5. difficult   10. giggle

Same Starts, page 71

1. stairs   5. long
2. beneath   6. jelly
3. aid   7. joyful
4. sign

Take Your Choice!, page 72

1. entertainment
2. motioned
3. damp
4. statue
5. witness
6. forecasted

Cross Synonym Puzzle, page 73

Across	Down
1. marriage	3. control
2. educate	8. rare
3. commercial	9. necessary
4. lawyer	10. attic
5. ancient	11. wit
6. pilot	
7. college	

A Bunch of Synonyms, page 74

1. annoys
2. amount
3. average
4. apprentice, ability
5. awkward, aisle
6. advice

True or False?, page 75

1. T
2. F — If you look at a thermometer, you can tell what the temperature is.
3. F — A hero is someone who is very brave.
4. T
5. F — A violet dress is a shade of purple.
6. T
7. T
8. F — An orchard of orange trees can also be called a grove.

Find the Synonyms, page 76

1. The bald dad is holding the bawling infant.
2. The coach was overjoyed since his team won the game.
3. All respected the heroine for her courageous behavior.
4. Sara's physician prescribed expensive tablets for her.

You Be the Writer!, page 77

1. A man is dozing on the couch. A man is sleeping on the sofa.
2. A woman is closing the drapes. A lady is drawing the curtains.
3. A monkey is in the cage. A chimp is in the cage.

It's in the Bag, page 78

1. annual   4. peculiar
2. resigned   5. ornaments
3. coaxed   6. fragments

If You Are..., page 79

1. yes
2. no — giggling
3. yes
4. no — injure
5. yes
6. no — funny

Three-Way Tricky Crosswords, page 80

1. laugh, giggle
2. diner, cafe
3. finish, end
4. display, show
5. instruct, teach
6. friend, partner

Answer Two Ways!, page 81

1. buying, purchasing
2. cabinet, cupboard
3. cemetery, graveyard

Synonyms

Three's a Charm, page 82

1. disaster
2. swap
3. perished
4. persuaded
5. fragile
6. substitute

Double Clues, page 83

1. missing
2. banner
3. hallway
4. error
5. immense
6. loss
7. occupation
8. gossip
9. stiffen
10. possess

Can You Match These?, page 84

1. courageous
2. rotates
3. employees
4. inhabitant
5. burglar
6. fatal
7. aloft
8. retrieves

Which of Three?, page 85

1. pedestrian
2. perspire
3. empty
4. surgery
5. garments
6. avalanche

Crossword Stumpers, page 86

1. denote, notice
2. think, study
3. luggage, bags
4. odor, fragrance
5. salary, wages
6. violet, purple

Your Turn to Write, page 87

1. enemy — Watch out for the enemy.
   foe — He is a dangerous foe.
2. dejected — She was dejected by the news.
   sad — He was sad to hear of his friend's loss.
3. altitude — We are climbing to a higher altitude.
   height — Take a measurement of his height.
4. expert — She is an expert in mathematics.
   specialist — He works as a specialist in the police department.
5. vault — Keep the jewels in the vault.
   safe — Be sure to lock the safe.

To Tell the Truth, page 88

1. T
2. F — When you're drowsy, you're sleepy.
3. T
4. T
5. F — If you're a beginner, you're an apprentice.
6. F — A lawyer presents evidence to a jury.
7. T
8. F — If you're joyful, you feel elated.

Be Creative!, page 89

Across
1. barricade
2. achievement
3. obtain
4. solution
5. lift

Down
6. edge
7. advise
8. draw
9. robbery
10. illegal

Semantic Absurdities

Right or Wrong?, page 92

1. Ducks do not wear rain gear.
2. They can't see the ball when playing at night.
3. Children are not allowed to drive cars.

Hear Ye, Hear Ye!, page 93

plant, sock, ball, balloon, rope, rock

Good Night, Nelson!, page 95

2, 3, 5, 6

Turkey Time, page 96

The chicken should be a cooked turkey.
The girl should sit on a chair, not a tire.
The mother should use a fork to eat, not a stick.
The ducks should be outside the house, not inside.
The train track should be on the floor, not the table.
The boy should eat from a plate, not a stop sign.

Zoo Mix-Up, page 97

1. A duck doesn't wear clothing.
2. A fish doesn't live in a doghouse.
3. A giraffe doesn't wear a saddle.
4. A zebra doesn't swim underwater.
5. A bird doesn't read a book.
6. A bear doesn't use paper and scissors.

A Photo Finish, page 98

1. Turtles are very slow.
2. Caterpillars are small and move short distances.
3. Elderly people move slowly.
4. Babies move short distances when crawling.

Family Trade-Off, page 99

1. Adults don't play with baby rattles.
2. The uniform doesn't fit.

3. Men do not wear decorated combs in their hair.
4. Little boys do not carry briefcases.
5. Adults do not ride tricycles.
6. Men do not carry women's purses.

Make It Right!, page 101

1. paper
2. hair
3. drink
4. square
5. water

Apple of My Eye, page 103

1. Nichole snores when she's asleep.
2. My grandmother makes good apple pies.
3. The mail gets to my house at noon.
4. I play baseball with a glove.
5. Baseball players sit on bleachers when they aren't playing.
6. My neighbor was angry when the kids danced in the yard.
7. We keep our toys and old furniture in the garage.
8. At lunchtime, I ate with a friend.

Appliance Barn, page 105

1. A mixer has beaters, not forks.
2. Burners are round.
3. A toaster has a button, not a clothespin.
4. A cord has a plug, not a flower.
5. A vacuum cleaner doesn't have headlights.
6. A refrigerator doesn't cook popcorn.

Let's Be Sensible, page 106

1. C, money
2. A, ladder
3. D, towel
4. E, clown
5. B, yell/cheer

Silly Sentences, page 107

1. People don't eat nails.
2. You buy plants at stores.
3. Basketballs are not painted.
4. People don't read irons.
5. People don't choose the weather.

Picture Match, page 108

1. D — People don't have beaks.
2. A — Children aren't allowed to drive.
3. E — People don't walk with their arms.

4. B — Pumpkins don't wear clothing.
5. C — Drains are not in drawers.

Fix Up, page 109

1. smell
2. flower
3. meal
4. celery
5. coast
6. bulldozer
7. dollars
8. borrow
9. destroyed
10. frowned
11. wound
12. hare

Strange Crosswords!, page 110

Across
1. emergency
2. damp
3. announced
4. deaf

Down
1. enormous
5. earned
6. cured
7. council
8. starved

It's Your Draw, page 111

1. The plane arrived at the airport.
2. A bird uses its beak to eat.
3. I sailed across the ocean in a ship.

Wrong Way!, page 112

1. You don't eat wood for dinner.
2. Fruits aren't greedy.
3. You don't celebrate when you lose something.
4. You don't brush your teeth with a paintbrush.
5. People don't live in caves.
6. Houses aren't in the harbor.
7. turkey, ham, roast beef
8. people
9. birthday, anniversary, holiday
10. paint something
11. bats, bears
12. ships, boats, tug boats

What a Pair!, page 113

1. X O
2. X O
3. X O
4. X O
5. O X
6. O X

Tic-Tac-Toe, page 114

1. O X X
2. O X O
3. X O X
4. O O X

You Don't Say!, page 115

1. courtyard — Jackie looked in her cookbook to find a good recipe for garlic chicken.
2. worthless — The ring was so valuable, Ben sold it for a thousand dollars.

Semantic Absurdities

You Don't Say!, page 115

3. geologist — The gardener planted the seeds by hand.
4. dungeon — The new baby slept in a crib.
5. batches — The large ranch has two hundred acres of land.
6. lasso — The horse's colt stood on its wobbly legs.
7. recall — Brent had to step on the brakes to avoid hitting the car in front of him.
8. loyal — Dee's toothache felt very painful.

Crossword Capers, page 116

Across	Down
1. custodian	1. commercial
2. gumdrops	6. beef
3. racket	7. innocent
4. nursery	8. trapeze
5. snore	9. pedal
6. blizzard	

Fool's Gold, page 117

1. Kara dawdles on her way to school, so she's always late.
2. When I gain weight, I weigh more than before.
3. I like to hear Randy sing, so I encourage him.
4. Ray was the narrator of the story, so he said a lot.
5. I prefer receiving an A grade instead of an F.
6. The tornado was expected after we heard the siren go off.
7. The teacher praised the boy for all his good work.
8. We rode the trolley to the other side of the city.

What a Laugh!, page 118

1. I eat cereal every morning for breakfast.
2. We saw a fish in the pet store aquarium.
3. The baseball player made a run just before time ran out.
4. A centipede is a caterpillar with many legs.
5. When it's 10° outside, I turn the furnace on to keep warm.
6. When you throw a pass, you're playing a game of football.
7. One of the ingredients in pizza is cheese.
8. During a hurricane, strong winds blow.
9. We rode the ferry across the river.
10. A baby horse is called a colt.

This Sounds Silly!, page 119

1. Giraffes don't have tusks. The young elephant already has tusks.
2. A compass doesn't mow grass. My uncle used a lawn mower to mow his grass.
3. Something sturdy doesn't collapse. The table was so wobbly it collapsed.
4. A tractor doesn't have a propeller. The airplane's propeller wouldn't move.
5. Lumber isn't used to make streets. The workers poured concrete to make new streets.
6. A sailboat is not ridden on the sidewalk. Sharon rides her bicycle on the sidewalk.

Wrap It Up, page 120

1. flattened	6. meteor
2. wallpaper	7. harp
3. locket	8. headband
4. pickup	9. windshield
5. citizen	10. cafe

Word Swap, page 121

1. The king lives in a castle.
2. We went to the arena to see the boxing match.
3. The surgeon decided to begin the delicate operation.
4. The soldier lifted the drawbridge to keep the enemies out.
5. The skyscraper has ninety floors.
6. The beggar's shack was falling apart.
7. The basketball player needed some refreshment after the tiring game.
8. The woman keeps her expensive jewels in a safe.

Tell Me Truthfully, page 122

1. T
2. F — You can cram clothing into a backpack.
3. F — When you broil something, you heat it.
4. T
5. F — We sleep on beds every night.
6. T
7. F — Petrified rock is hard and powdery.
8. F — A police officer could arrest a robber.

Hot Fudge Sundae!, page 123

1. An apron protects clothes when cooking.
3. A spoon is used to eat ice cream.
5. It will melt.
7. Barbeque sauce wouldn't taste good on ice cream.
8. Other fruit will taste better, such as pineapple.
9. A rope won't open a container.
11. You don't measure cherries with a teaspoon.
13. You don't eat ice cream with chopsticks.

Change Up, page 124

1. correct
2. trim
3. mechanic
4. fabric
5. ambulance
6. snowstorm
7. rodent
8. behavior
9. hockey
10. wobbly

Cross-Wise, page 125

1. ripen; thaw
2. album; cookbook
3. dairy; store
4. bun; bowl
5. sour; cold
6. navigate; plant
7. wastebasket; cat
8. pizza; drink
9. sandpaper; blankets
10. quarts; miles

W	T	C	P	I	Z	Z	A	R
A	T	M	J	K	N	Y	O	N
S	A	N	D	P	A	P	E	R
T	F	U	L	A	V	P	G	A
E	P	K	V	Y	I	H	O	L
B	U	H	J	R	G	R	W	B
A	Z	Q	W	S	A	D	Y	U
S	O	U	R	X	T	B	A	M
K	D	B	O	C	E	R	C	K
E	X	Q	U	A	R	T	S	H
T	L	Z	I	N	S	V	H	E

Trading Places, page 126

1. stroller	5. peacock
2. pitchfork	6. funnel
3. alternate	7. illegal
4. tollbooth	8. dishwasher

Patch-work, page 127

1. The shuttle took the astronauts to their spacecraft.
2. Last year, we took our summer vacation on a yacht.
3. A triceratops is a kind of dinosaur.
4. I got a postcard in the mail from my cousin.
5. Judy has a math exam next Tuesday.
6. We gathered a bushel of apples from one tree.

That's Absurd!, page 128

1. The incense had a terrible smell.
2. Mom wrote a check to purchase our tickets for the play.
3. The detective completed the investigation when he caught the thief.
4. My savings account declined when I withdrew money from it.
5. In the summer, we usually get a lot of heat.
6. The piano solo was so bad that the audience didn't applaude.
7. Karen was a patient in the hospital for two weeks after her car accident.
8. When Andrew's stereo blared, his neighbors always heard it.

School Days, page 129

Jon attended school every day last year, so he got a perfect attendance award.
This year, he'll learn about multiplication and division.
Nonfiction fascinates Jon because he knows what he's reading is true.
He usually cleans the erasers and washes the chalkboard.
When he gets home, Jon starts his homework.

Dictionary Disgrace, page 130

1. pledge	6. abbreviation
2. jubilant	7. griddle
3. sapphire	8. salary
4. vital	9. fatigue
5. wed	10. persist

Crossword Comedy, page 131

Across	Down
1. spectator	1. swiveled
2. somber	7. tropical
3. revived	8. juvenile
4. souvenirs	9. bleach
5. chaos	10. denim
6. foes	11. spat

Antonyms

Quiet or Noisy?, page 136

quiet — 3, 5, 6
noisy — 1, 2, 4, 7, 8

Make a Choice, page 137

1. get presents
2. fix it
3. whisper

Antonyms

Cactus Facts, page 140

1. dry
2. deserts
3. near
4. catch
5. outside
6. thin
7. thick
8. desert
9. best

Munch, Munch!, page 141

soft — 1, 3, 6, 8, 9
crunchy — 2, 4, 5, 7, 10

Match These Opposites, page 143

1. ugly
2. dirty
3. cold
4. dry
5. far
6. no
7. yes
8. yes
9. no
10. no

Crazy Computer, page 144

1. Aunt
2. sending
3. my
4. glad
5. buy
6. friends
7. love
8. after
9. day
10. new
11. tomorrow
12. fine
13. thank you
14. wonderful
15. nephew

What's Special about Siberia, page 145

1. northern
2. always
3. coldest
4. lowest
5. below
6. cold
7. good
8. First
9. fresh
10. cold
11. healthy

Opposites Attract, page 146

1. slower
2. straight
3. late
4. right
5. spends
6. sour
7. send
8. dull
9. plain
10. follow

Which Melts Faster?, page 147

1. clean
2. faster
3. Clean
4. frozen
5. white
6. white
7. light
8. Dirty
9. dark
10. melt
11. faster
12. dirty
13. melts
14. clean

Choices, Choices!, page 149

1. strong
2. public
3. graceful
4. unknown
5. colorful
6. create

Sense and Nonsense, page 150

1. A dragon is make-believe.
2. An ocean is deep.
3. A football field is wide.
4. A candle is solid.
5. We punish criminals.
6. Lightning is visible.
7. A whisper is quiet.
8. A brick sinks in water.
9. A pencil is straight.
10. A diamond is shiny.

Silly Seth, page 151

1. frowns
2. subtracts
3. spends
4. yells
5. disobeys
6. nervous
7. playful
8. right
9. lie
10. rapidly

What's It All About?, page 152

1. nearby.
2. the nearest house.
3. at sunset.
4. southern.
5. in the center.

Crossword Opposites, page 153

Across
1. wife
2. sun
3. dangerous
4. upper
5. false
6. float
7. narrow

Down
1. wonderful
8. modern
9. truth
10. leader

Opposites!, page 154

1. gentle
2. frown
3. unknown
4. crunchy
5. fancy
6. sturdy
7. famine
8. solid
9. most
10. deep

No Nonsense!, page 155

1. aloud
2. proud
3. dangerous
4. dawn
5. difficult
6. difference
7. encourage
8. true

Match 'em Up!, page 156

princess, beautiful; beast, ugly
ocean, deep; brook, shallow
star, bright; clay, dull
satin, smooth; nail file, rough
elephant, enormous; mouse, tiny
correct, right; mistaken, wrong
UFO, strange; jet, ordinary
acid, harsh; lotion, mild

Crossword Fun!, page 157

Across
1. together
2. remember
3. outside
4. left
5. ugly
6. ahead

Down
7. evening
8. brother
9. below
10. front

What's the Meaning of This?, page 158

1. read it silently.
2. where the water is deep.
3. a club anyone can join.
4. a permanent address.
5. a sunny place.

Sunken Treasure, page 159

1. punish
2. sad
3. calm
4. defend
5. unknown
6. famine
7. messy
8. soggy
9. solid
10. rear

The Frogfish, page 160

1. rare
2. catches
3. long
4. outside
5. end
6. prey
7. floats
8. smaller
9. tiny

Take Your Pick!, page 161

1. similar
2. tighten
3. mild
4. lengthy
5. nearest
6. Honest
7. harmful
8. scarce
9. protect
10. buyer

Choose Your Opposites, page 162

1. punish
2. sunny
3. accept
4. tidy
5. playful
6. harm
7. common
8. soften
9. cause
10. failure

You Be The Judge!, page 163

1. unfamiliar
2. answer
3. fat
4. brittle
5. scarce
6. brave
7. endanger
8. brief
9. ascend
10. future
11. awkward
12. planned

Leaping Opposites, page 164

1. thin
2. best
3. hero
4. wife
5. real
6. wild
7. bend
8. soften
9. public

Crazy Cooking!, page 165

1. heat
2. boils
3. add
4. melts
5. combine
6. dry
7. large
8. sharp
9. wet
10. gently
11. soft
12. smooth
13. divide
14. half
15. rise
16. warm
17. top
18. cool

Match the Opposites, page 166

1. A
2. C
3. O
4. K
5. E
6. R
7. P
8. D
9. L

A COCKER POODLE DOO

Find the Opposite, page 167

1. basement
2. teacher
3. reject
4. melt
5. strong
6. sell
7. temporary
8. praise
9. minus
10. calm

Do You Have a Match?, page 168

1. c
2. k
3. e
4. l
5. b
6. j
7. a
8. g
9. flood
10. blend
11. foreign
12. separate
13. national
14. arrest

Make It Make Sense!, page 169

1. fertile
2. arrest
3. shrink
4. fresh
5. lengthen
6. weary
7. loosen
8. celebrate

Sentence Sense, page 171

1. passenger
2. nephew
3. villain
4. Urban
5. niece
6. restrain
7. pedestrian
8. rural
9. release
10. hero

Double Your Answer!, page 172

1. antique
2. sell
3. multiply
4. horizontal
5. soggy
6. disappear
7. bright
8. delicate
9. brighten
10. create
11. soggy
12. disappear
13. create
14. sell
15. antique
16. delicate
17. bright
18. multiply
19. brighten
20. horizontal

Make a Choice!, page 173

1. barren
2. contracts
3. vowel
4. ferocious
5. interior
6. clean
7. an amateur
8. rural
9. absent
10. conceals

Definitions

The Bird Is the Word, page 176

1. yes
2. eat
3. no
4. no
5. yes
6. yes
7. yes
8. no

ANSWER KEY

Definitions

Clowning Around, page 177

1. bright clothes, funny hats, wigs, make-up
2. no — Some are sad because they have lost something or for other reasons.
3. Yes, because they want to make people laugh.
4. ride in tiny cars, throw pies, pop balloons, juggle
5. circus, parties, fairs
6. yes — They are real people who are wearing costumes.

Bear-y Good Words, page 178

1. true: ears, claws, fur, tails
   not true: antlers, wings
2. true: growl, chew, run
   not true: drive, whistle, write

My New Coat, page 179

1. wear it
2. button, zip, tie
3. when it's cold or rainy
4. anyone
5. to keep warm and dry
6. outside

In the Swim, page 180

1. kick
2. no — There is no oxygen to breathe.
3. no — You might need help from someone.
4. bathing suit
5. no — You will hit bottom and hurt yourself.

Way Up High, page 181

1. mountains — They are large and can be several thousand feet high.
3. airplane — It can fly high in the air.
4. flag — It can be raised high in the air on a pole.
6. cloud — It is located high in the sky.

My Best Friend is..., page 182

1. yes   3. yes
2. yes   4. no

1. I'm sorry
2. talks and listens
3. hugs
4. lets you know she wants to help

Happy Birthday!, page 186

Across	Down
1. shoe	6. sidewalk
2. eagle	7. pencil
3. sandwich	8. orange
4. lamb	
5. oven	

Yes or No?, page 187

1. yes	2. yes	3. no
yes	yes	yes
no	no	yes
no	yes	no

Flower Fun, page 188

1. alike   5. dove
2. belt   6. creek
3. kitchen   7. basement
4. center   8. Earth

Round Up, page 189

1. great   6. over
2. hint   7. frequently
3. little   8. pitch
4. thief   9. blossom
5. bucket

You're a Star Student!, page 190

1. wins   3. chases
2. tiptoes   4. tears

Can This Be True?, page 191

1. X
   X
   O — You wash your hair with shampoo.
2. X
   O — A pillow is soft.
   O — Pillows go on the bed.
3. X
   O — A bench is wider than a chair.
   X
4. X
   O — A bus is a large vehicle.
   X
5. O — An elevator takes you from one floor to another.
   O — Several people can ride an elevator at a time.
   X

Write It Out, page 192

1. A ladder has rungs and is used to climb up or down something.
2. A nest is made of twigs and is a bird's home in a tree.
3. A piano is a musical instrument with many keys.
4. An island is a piece of land surrounded by water.

Ready for Riddles?, page 193

1. nut   4. alligator
2. kangaroo   5. attic
3. lights   6. curtain

Puzzle Fun!, page 194

Across	Down
1. kangaroo	6. motor
2. pollution	7. acorn
3. repeat	8. gull
4. fin	9. beak
5. rent	10. ticket
	11. neat

Match Me, page 195

1. h   6. i
2. g   7. b
3. e   8. c
4. a   9. d
5. j   10. f

What Does It Mean?, page 196

1. He felt guilty because what he did was wrong.
2. She was responsible for the broken window.
3. The children were anxious for school to start.
4. The students went for a long walk.
5. The floor had some fluid on it, maybe water or juice.
6. The teacher meant, "Speak clearly."

Storytelling Fun, page 197

1. many people who also came to hear the group play
2. creases and puckers
3. fell down
4. on sale
5. the man who directs the orchestra
6. a group of people who play musical instruments together

Which Is Which?, page 199

1. fossil   5. fake
2. furniture   6. rescue
3. holiday   7. symbol
4. create   8. hive

Sort It Out, page 200

1. statue   5. opponent
2. opinion   6. coward
3. witness   7. century
4. physician   8. companion

Check It Out!, page 201

1. blizzard   4. auditorium
2. cabbage   5. screwdriver
3. actor   6. strawberry

Be a Word Wizard!, page 202

Across	Down
1. flavor	6. file
2. limb	6. rumor
3. source	7. trophy
4. boulder	8. shrub
5. antique	9. advice

What Does It Mean?, page 203

1. advances   5. write
2. bother   6. hesitate
3. confess   7. observe
4. connect   8. release

Match 'em Up!, page 204

1. hard to believe
2. not done on purpose
3. spooky or scary
4. from many countries
5. normal
6. dangerous or unhealthy
7. of the highest quality
8. confused

Crazy Riddles!, page 205

1. D, I, N   4. B, G, K
2. E, J, O   5. A, H, M
3. C, F, L

Wright the Right Choice, page 206

1. brief — I caught a glimpse of the mayor when we passed his car.
2. competes — My opponent will be tough to beat.
3. tells — The narrator speaks with a clear voice.
4. scary — I was shaking from the nightmare.
5. answer — I just thought of a solution to your problem.
6. wet — The ducks will nest in the marsh.
7. guess — I have a hunch you're right.
8. argument — The quarrel was about politics.

Be Descriptive, page 207

1. is not afraid.
2. it is short in length.
3. has lost the hair on his head.
4. is very thin.
5. is delicate.
6. is not graceful.
7. it will not hurt you.
8. is ongoing without change.

Could These Be True?, page 208

1. F — The huge clock in the dining room is very noisy.
2. T
3. F — The strong weightlifter won the championship.

264

ANSWER KEY

Definitions

4. F — Mother's spaghetti sauce simmered on the stove.
5. T
6. T
7. F — Molly and Ben took the elevator to the top of the skyscraper.
8. T

Pair These Up, page 209

1. c   5. b
2. j   6. i
3. f   7. d
4. a   8. g

What Does It Mean?, page 210

Across
1. petrified
2. wed
3. location
4. possess
5. fertilizer
6. remedy
7. baggage

Down
4. pretzel
5. fume
8. fawn
9. drowsy
10. arctic

Choose the Best, page 211

1. conference   5. tractor
2. bruise   6. plantation
3. chandelier   7. reminder
4. charcoal   8. hammock

Which of These?, page 212

1. T
2. F — Monica studied all night for the semester exam.
3. F — The bridge was supported by two strong cables over the canyon.
4. T
5. T
6. F — Sally's new pen leaked and the ink spread on the paper.
7. T
8. F — After landing on the beach, the army invaded the island.
9. F — Everyone drove their vehicles through the intersection.
10. T

You Be the Dictionary, page 213

1. suitcases — Put the luggage on the plane.
2. carry — He will tote the sack of groceries.
3. someone who is traveling by walking — The pedestrian looked carefully before crossing the road.
4. cook slowly just below the boiling point — Please simmer the stew.

All in a Day's Work, page 214

1. sheriff   5. pitchfork
2. badge   6. jackrabbit
3. saddlebags   7. raven
4. canteen   8. criminals

Name that Picture, page 215

1. skateboard — I like to ride my skateboard.
2. binoculars — He used binoculars to watch the game.
3. submarine — The submarine was under water for days.
4. funnel — She poured the mixture into the funnel.

Multiple Definitions

Pick a Pair of Friends, page 218

bat: A bat is used to hit balls when playing. baseball. A bat has wings and can fly.
trip: People are traveling by car while on an overnight trip. The board made him trip and fall.
box: A present is in the box. He's wearing gloves to box.

Big Wheel, page 225

land: Planes land on runways. This land is called the coast.
pen: A pig lives in a pen. You write a letter with a pen.
tie: You can wear a tie with a shirt. People tie their shoes.
straw: The straw is kept in a barn. You can drink from a cup with a straw.

Hare Today, Gone Tomorrow, page 227

march: March is the month after February and before April. Children march in a parade.
nut: He is acting like a nut. You can eat a nut.
bowl: You can mix things in a bowl. She throws the ball when it's her turn to bowl.

Let It Snow, page 228

stick: A stick is part of a bush or a tree. Gum will stick to your shoe.
steps: Steps are stairs used to walk up or down an incline. He makes steps with his feet.
watch: She can watch with her eyes. You wear a watch to know the time.

miss: A young girl is called a miss. A boy will miss and not catch the ball thrown to him.

Super Shopper, page 229

1. part   5. ground
2. feed   (beef)
3. ground   6. feed
4. part

Who Sees What?, page 231

shot: Someone shot an arrow. A photographer shot a picture.
slip: A slip is something you wear. You can slip on a wet floor.
snap: A snap is a noise. A snap is a fastener to hold something together.

School Days, School Days, page 232

pipe: Water drains down the pipe from the sink. Some people smoke a pipe.
shade: A shade keeps light from coming in the window. Trees give shade by blocking light from the sun.
horn: A bull has horns. Blow the horn.

Snow Fort Fun, page 233

bill: A bird's beak is called a bill. A bill from a store tells you an amount of money that is owed.
brush: A brush is used to make hair look neat. Brush grows on the land.
wave: A wave is made by movements in the water. People wave their hands to say hello or goodbye.
plain: A large, flat area of land is a plain. A Valentine that is not decorated is plain.

Dandy Designs, page 234

cast: throw; make a knot or stitch
steer: guide; young ox
batter: beat; a mixture of flour, egg, and milk or water

Climbing The Walls, page 235

bulb: plant; something round or swollen
stamp: pound; mark or paper on a letter to show that postage has been paid
coast: glide or move smoothly; land near the shore

Pots o' Words, page 236

pitcher: The pitcher throws the ball to the batter in the baseball game. You can pour a drink from a pitcher.
palm: A palm tree is very tall. A palm is part of a hand.
hood: The hood of a jacket goes over your head. The hood of a car protects engine.

Title Two-somes!, page 237

The San Francisco Bay The bay is a small area of water near San Francisco. The book may be about the water and land in that area.

Bay at the Moon To bay means to make a howling sound. The book may be about an animal that howls at the moon.

They Faint When They're Frightened People can become unconscious when they are afraid. The book may be about people who do this.

The Mystery of the Faint Diary Writing that has faded is faint. This book may be about a diary that is difficult to read because the writing is faded.

Seal the Box, Wendy To seal a box, you close it and make the closing secure by using tape or glue. This book may be about a girl who puts something in a box and closes it securely.

The Baby Seal A seal is an animal that lives in the ocean. This book may be about one of these animals that is very young.

Charlotte's Web, page 238

1. A beam of light help you see in the dark.
2. You can hang things from a beam of wood.
3. Put film in your camera to take a picture.
4. They are here to film a movie.
5. Play the record on the stereo.
6. I want to record him on tape.
7. My broken arm is in a cast.
8. The actress in the play is a member of the cast.

ANSWER KEY

Multiple Definitions

The Great Frame-Up, page 239

fan: a machine that cools the air; a supporter or admirer
quarter: one-fourth; a coin which has a value of twenty-five cents
scale: object that measures weight; climb
check: a mark; a written paper used to pay someone

Flag Day, page 240

buck: One dollar is called a buck. A male deer is called a buck.
picket: A picket fence is made of many boards. They carry signs as they picket the zoo.
sole: Sole is a kind of fish. The bottom of a shoe is the sole.

Photographer's Nightmare, page 241

1. calf: The calf is the lower part of the leg.
2. diamond: A diamond is a shape made of four straight lines.
3. diamond: A diamond is a precious stone or gem.
4. calf: A baby cow is called a calf.
5. jacks: Jacks are small and pointed, and are used in a game.
6. jack: A jack is used to lift a car.

Alien Alert!, page 242

admit: allow someone to enter; agree that something is true
clipper: something that cuts; a ship
brim: edge; rim of a hat
date: a fruit; when something will happen
limb: leg or arm of a person; branch of a tree

Wheeler Dealer, page 243

racket: noise; something used to hit a ball
pupil: student; part of the eye
channel: part of a river; a frequency of a radio or television signal
bluff: cliff; deceive someone
dough: money; a flour mixture used in baking

Prehistoric Picture Match, page 244

grave: The body was placed in a grave. The situation is grave.

organ: He plays the organ. The kidney is an organ.
mint: I ate a mint. He picked some mint from the garden.

Computer Mania, page 245

flatter: I flatter my mom when I say I like her cooking. The tire is flatter today than it was yesterday.
uniform: The police officer wears a uniform. The bricks were lined in uniform.
tick: A tick bit my dog. The clock has a loud tick.

The WORD Award, page 246

barge: He towed the barge down the river. Please don't barge into my room like that.
coaster: She rode the roller coaster twenty times. Putting the glass on a coaster will protect the table.
bun: She put her long hair in a bun. The bun was stale.

The WORD Search, page 247

B	L	Q	U	O	V	Y	U	D
T	I	S	S	U	E	M	I	D
S	A	R	F	T	O	Z	R	P
W	H	P	E	L	T	A	Y	B
X	G	C	Z	E	F	H	J	K
J	M	O	N	T	I	S	U	E

hail: greet; rain that is made of small clumps of ice
tissue: soft paper; parts of plants or animals
outlet: stream from a lake; place where you plug or unplug electrical appliances
pelt: skin of an animal; throw
draft: draw; select

Multiple Meaning Crossword, page 248

Across
1. chaps: The chaps are coming for tea.
2. camper: He is a good camper.
3. surf: I like to swim in the surf.

Down
1. chaps: His chaps are worn from riding.
4. camper: sleep in the camper.
5. surf: I want to learn to surf.

A Better Idea, page 249

brand: I don't like that brand of soup. It takes a lot of work to brand a cow.
current: Watch the news to see what's current. He's swimming in the current.
cable: My mother wants to send a cable to my father. I like to ride the cable cars in San Francisco.
trial: I have the book on a free trial basis. The lawyer has a trial in court today.

Directory Assistance, page 250

bristle: He will bristle in anger. The cat's fur is like bristle.
gorge: We hiked through the gorge. She is so hungry she will gorge herself at lunch.
spruce: There is a spruce tree growing in my yard. To look nice, she will spruce herself up.

bureau: I keep my sweaters in the bureau. He will report the information to people at the bureau.
petrified: She is petrified at the thought of losing her money. The wood has petrified and is like stone.

Let's Play Basketball, page 251

tart mow console cuff

Skateboard Sanchez, page 252

1. appointment: designation; engagement
2. decline: refuse; go down
3. cavity: hollow space; tooth decay
4. combination: things put together; numbers in a specific order

Double Strength, page 253

1. dribble: trickle of liquid; bounce a basketball several times
2. derby: a race; a hat

3. sow: pig; to plant seeds
4. clutter: many objects scattered and disordered; noise or disturbance

Postcard Homework, page 254

1. ball.
2. about the accident.
3. when we were fishing.
4. to begin her routine.
5. because I'm not interested.
6. came from the garage.
7. needs to be cleaned.
8. is forty cents.
9. is underground.
10. is steep.

Sign Up, page 255

1. flounder: a fish; to struggle (U.S. highway sign)
2. fuse: cord to an explosive device; melt together (speed limit sign)
3. draft: flow of air; draw or write (interstate highway sign)
4. depression: feeling sad; hollow or low place (stop sign)
5. yield: give up or surrender; give way to someone else (yield sign)

Cinco de Mayo, page 256

furrow: The plow made a furrow in the field. Don't furrow your forehead!
canteen: Buy your lunch in the canteen. Carry the canteen on your belt.
relish: Have some relish on your hotdog. He will relish the idea of going on vacation.
pinto: I ate pinto beans for lunch. I want to ride the pinto.

Bubble Trouble, page 257

1. minor: small; not important
2. manual: work with the hands; guidebook
3. formal: a dance; something done according to custom or rules
4. sling: throw; a bandage

266

Copyright © 1988 LinguiSystems, Inc.

WORD LIST

Grade K - 1

after
always
apple
back
bad
bag
ball
bark
bat
bear
beautiful
because
bed
bee
best
big
bike
bird
birthday
black
blue
boat
book
box
breakfast
brother
brown
bus
cake
car
cat
cave
chair
children
city
clean
cloud
clown
coat
cold
cook
cow
cry
dad
dance
dark
day
dinner
doctor
dog
door
draw
drink
drove
duck
eat
end
every
everyone
eye
face
fall
family
far
fast
father
feed
feet
fill
fine
first
fish
fix
floor

flower
fly
food
friend
frog
game
girl
glad
glass
good
grass
great
green
grow
guess
happy
hat
hear
heard
help
high
horse
hot
house
how
hurt
in
inside
kind
king
kitten
lake
last
laugh
leaves
leg
letter
light
line
little
long
lost
love
lunch
man
mean
miss
mix
money
morning
most
mother
mouse
my
near
new
night
noise
nose
now
on
outside
over
painting
paper
part
people
picture
pig
place
plant
play
pound

pretty
quiet
rabbit
rain
read
red
ride
right
road
rock
room
rope
run
sad
said
same
sandy
saw
sea
secret
see
seed
shoe
shop
shout
show
side
sign
sing
sister
sky
sleep
slow
small
smell
smile
sorry
squirrel
step
stick
stone
store
sun
swim
tail
tall
teacher
tell
thank
tiger
tire
together
top
toy
track
train
tree
trick
turtle
TV
under
watch
water
wet
what
when
where
white
who
why
window
winter
woman
wood

work
yellow
your
zoo

Grade 2

above
across
add
afraid
agree
ahead
airplane
alike
angry
answer
apart
apartment
arm
asleep
aunt
baby
balloon
band
bank
barn
baseball
basement
basket
beach
bedroom
before
behind
below
belt
bench
beside
between
bill
blackberry
blanket
bloom
body
boot
bottle
bottom
bought
bowl
branch
brave
bread
break
bright
brook
brush
bug
buildings
bump
bunch
burn
butter
buy
cage
candle
cap
careful
carrot
carry
castle
catch
center
chase
cheese
cherry

chest
chew
chicken
child
chirp
choose
circle
circus
classroom
clay
clear
cloth
clothes
clue
cool
corn
cost
crab
crash
crayon
cross
cup
curl
daylight
deer
detective
dirt
dish
dive
doghouse
doll
dollar
done
doorbell
doorway
dragon
dream
dress
drew
drive
driver
during
ear
early
earth
easy
egg
elevator
enemy
fact
farm
farmer
fat
favorite
feather
fence
field
finish
float
flood
flour
follow
foot
forest
fruit
fur
gallop
garage
garden
gate
grade
grandfather
grandmother
growl
hammer
hang

hard
heavy
horn
hospital
hug
huge
island
jam
jet
job
joy
key
kid
kitchen
ladder
lady
large
late
leaf
library
lie
lift
listen
log
lunchtime
machine
mail
march
mask
meadow
measure
middle
milk
mirror
monkey
month
mountain
nail
neighbor
nest
newspaper
notice
number
nut
ocean
office
often
once
orange
oven
overhead
owl
own
pail
paintings
pant
paste
path
paw
pea
pen
pencil
penny
phone
piano
picnic
pie
piece
pillow
pin
pink
pipe
plain
plane
plate
player

WORD LIST

Grade 2

playground
pole
police
pond
pony
poor
popcorn
potato
present
puppy
purple
puzzle
raccoon
radio
ring
river
roar
robber
rode
roll
roof
rose
rough
row
ruler
sack
safe
sand
sandwich
sank
save
scare
scary
second
sense
shade
sharp
shell
shine
ship
shirt
shoot
shore
short
shot
shy
sick
sidewalk
silly
silver
sink
skate
slide
slip
smart
smooth
snap
sock
soft
soil
spin
spring
stage
stair
stare
stove
straight
strange
straw
stream
stripe
summer
sunny
swing

team
tear
teeth
telephone
thin
through
tiny
tiptoe
toast
tool
toss
trail
trap
true
wagon
warm
wash
wear
weather
whisper
whistle
win
wing
wonder
worm
wrong
young

Grade 3

acorn
action
admire
adult
aid
airport
aloud
ancient
anger
announce
anxious
arrive
ash
ashamed
attack
attic
audience
August
author
autumn
award
awful
ballet
banana
banquet
bargain
basketball
bathroom
bathtub
batter
beak
beam
beast
behave
beneath
berry
bicycle
birch
biscuit
blame
blind
blood
borrow
bother
bounce

breathe
brick
bucket
buggy
bulb
bulldozer
cab
cactus
calm
camera
canoe
capture
carve
cast
catcher
celebrate
chalk
champion
check
cheese
chip
chose
claw
cliff
closet
club
coast
coffee
colorful
comb
common
complain
computer
conductor
confuse
control
correct
council
courage
court
cream
create
creek
crisp
crocodile
crook
crunch
cure
curtain
daisy
damp
dangerous
dawn
deaf
delicate
demand
desert
dial
dictionary
difference
difficult
dim
dime
diner
dinnertime
dinosaur
direct
direction
discourage
discuss
distance
dove
drain
drawer
dresser
dull

dusk
eager
eagle
earn
electric
electricity
emergency
encourage
engine
enormous
entrance
escape
examine
excitedly
excuse
exper
faint
fairy
false
familiar
famous
fan
fancy
faraway
fasten
feast
fierce
film
fin
firewood
fireworks
fireplace
flag
flashlight
flavor
flute
football
fork
forward
fossil
freedom
friendship
frighten
frown
furniture
gas
gentle
gift
giggle
giraffe
glove
glue
graceful
grain
grandpa
greed
grin
grind
grip
guard
gull
gun
haircut
harbor
hare
harm
harness
headlights
hero
highway
hike
hint
hive
hobby
holiday
hollow

homesick
honor
hoof
husband
ice cream
ill
insect
instant
instrument
invisible
iron
jacket
jail
jelly
jewel
joyful
juice
June
jungle
kangaroo
knife
lamb
lamp
leader
least
leopard
less
lettuce
lid
limp
liquid
lowered
magazine
make-believe
maple
match
meal
medicine
mess
metal
midnight
mistake
modern
motion
motor
mumble
munch
museum
musician
mystery
narrow
neat
necklace
needle
nervous
nickle
noisy
northern
nurse
oak
oat
odd
onion
opposite
orchestra
ordinary
paintbrush
pajama
palm
parent
partner
passenger
petal
photograph
pill
pilot

pine
pitch
pitcher
planet
playful
poison
policeman
pollution
post
powder
powdery
pride
princess
private
protect
public
puddle
pumpkin
punish
purse
quarter
quit
rapid
rare
rattle
rear
receive
recipe
record
refrigerator
regard
relax
rent
repeat
rescue
restaurant
ribbon
rider
rip
ripe
robin
row boat
rubber
ruin
saddle
sadness
scale
scissors
seal
season
secretary
serious
shallow
shortstop
silence
silent
simple
singer
skunk
snack
soda
solid
southern
spine
spoil
sport
squint
startle
starve
steam
stair
study
stumble
success
swamp
sweat

Grade 3

sweat
symbol
tame
theater
thick
thief
thrown
ticket
treasure
trim
trombone
tune
underground
underwater
upper
vacation
violin
visitor
walrus
war
watermelon
weight
western
wheat
worst
wound
wrinkle
yarn
yesterday
yum

Grade 4

ability
accidental
ancestor
acre
actor
addition
admit
advance
advertisement
advice
advise
afloat
aisle
album
alert
amount
amusement
annoy
antique
antler
ape
apprentice
argument
armchair
auditorium
average
avoid
awkward
backbone
bacon
bald
barber
batch
battery
beaten
beef
beet
beggar
bewildered
bitter

blizzard
blossom
blueberry
bluff
bold
bony
boulder
brief
brim
brittle
bronze
cabbage
calf
camel
cane
cannon
career
caterpillar
cement
centipede
century
championship
channel
chick
chimpanzee
citizen
clipper
cloudburst
clumsy
colt
comic
communicate
companion
compass
compete
confess
connect
contain
convince
cookbook
couch
counter
courtyard
coward
crib
crimson
current
custodian
dainty
date
daybreak
decoration
defeat
destroy
detest
diamond
disease
dislike
display
ditch
diver
dolphin
dough
doughnut
drape
drought
dungeon
eastern
educate
eerie
elm
emotion
endanger
entertainment
excellent
exhibit

eyebrow
farthest
ferry
file
flatter
flavor
forecast
freeze
fuel
furnace
gallon
gardener
gasoline
geologist
gesture
glimpse
goal
grave
guilt
gulf
gumdrop
hallway
harmful
harmless
harsh
health
height
hesitate
hitch
honest
hunch
hurricane
icicle
identify
ignore
incredible
independence
ingredient
inning
innocent
international
inventor
jacks
ladybug
lasso
lawyer
leak
lend
limb
liver
loosen
lumber
macaroni
magnify
mammal
marsh
marshmallow
mild
mill
mitten
mixture
moist
monument
mosquito
moth
muffin
narrator
necessary
nephew
nightmare
nursery
observe
October
odor
old-fashioned
opinion

opponent
orchard
organ
painful
pardon
pedal
permanent
phrase
physician
picket
plug
portrait
postcard
pounce
praise
propeller
pudding
pupil
quarrel
racket
radish
raincoat
raindrop
raspberry
raw
recall
relative
release
responsible
retreat
rotten
rumor
scarce
scent
screwdriver
select
seller
shower
shrub
similar
slavery
snout
sofa
sole
solution
source
spaghetti
sparrow
spear
squash
starry
statue
stool
strawberry
sturdy
suggestion
suitcase
sunrise
sunset
tackle
temperature
thanksgiving
thunderstorm
tighten
trapeze
trapper
triceratops
trolley
turquoise
tusk
unexpected
unknown
vacuum
valuable
vinegar
visible

volunteer
weapon
whisk
wildcat
witness
wolves
wrestler
yo-yo
zebra

Grade 5

adobe
adore
aloft
ambulance
annual
applaud
arctic
arena
arrest
auto
baggage
bandit
banner
barbecue
barge
behavior
blare
blot
bough
bracelet
brand
bridle
bristle
broil
broth
bruise
bun
bureau
buyer
cabinet
cable
cafe
calendar
campaign
camper
cavern
celery
cemetery
chandelier
chap
charcoal
chat
chemistry
chimp
chopstick
chortle
coarse
coaster
coax
collapse
collie
combination
competition
conclude
conference
consent
console
container
corridor
courtroom
criminal
cupboard
dairy

defend
dependable
dessert
devour
diary
disaster
dishonest
disobey
dome
dominoes
doubtful
draft
drawbridge
easygoing
embrace
error
evidence
exhibition
expand
fabric
fawn
filth
filthy
flatten
flexible
fluid
foul
fragile
fragment
freezer
frontier
fume
genuine
gorge
gossip
grate
gratitude
grieve
hail
hammock
harp
headband
hippopotamus
hockey
hoofbeats
hoop
horseshoe
humorous
husk
immense
inquire
instruct
jewelry
lab
ladle
lariat
legal
lily
lime
locket
loss
mason
mattress
maze
mechanic
medium
menu
meteor
morsel
mow
navigate
necktie
occupation
operation
ornament
orphan

WORD LIST

Grade 5

outlet
overcoat
parlor
pavement
pear
peculiar
pelican
pelt
penguin
perish
persuade
petrified
photo
physical
pickup
pier
piglet
pizza
plantation
plentiful
porpoise
porridge
possess
predict
pretzel
prey
pursue
pursuit
quart
refreshment
rehearsal
rely
reminder
reptile
research
resign
resume
rodent
rudder
sauce
scholar
scuba
shack
shrivel
shuttle
simmer
skyscraper
slack
snicker
snowstorm
soggy
sombrero
soothe
soybean
specimen
steak
stiffen
stingy
substitute
subtract
surgeon
surrender
survive
swap
swat
technique
thieves
toothbrush
tornado
tournament
tractor
transistor
trout
wallpaper

wastebasket
wharf
wheelbarrow
windshield
withdrew
wobbly
woodchuck
worthless

Grade 6

abbreviation
abdomen
accomplishment
acquire
alternate
altitude
amber
ambitious
applesauce
apricot
attorney
baboon
badge
banister
barrier
bass
bathrobe
battleship
binoculars
bleach
blouse
bonfire
boost
briefcase
brink
burglar
burner
bushel
cafeteria
canteen
caribou
cavity
chaos
charity
chemist
cherish
clutter
collage
collide
comrade
cooperate
cornmeal
courageous
cyclone
decline
denim
depression
derby
dishwasher
dismissal
disposal
division
downpour
drab
dribble
drizzle
drowsy
earmuffs
Easter
employee
enthusiastic
erase
erupt
exam

factor
falcon
fatal
fatigue
fingernail
flounder
foal
foe
forlorn
formal
fortress
fragrance
funnel
furrow
fuse
gauge
glum
griddle
grill
grinder
hesitant
ideal
igloo
illegal
illlustrate
incense
inhabitant
instructor
investigation
islander
jackrabbit
janitor
jellyfish
jubilant
juvenile
laser
lavender
lengthen
luggage
mantel
manual
mesh
migration
mink
minor
missile
mobile
monarch
motorcycle
muffler
muskrat
muzzle
navigator
nectar
nonfiction
nourish
observatory
observer
ore
outlandish
parallel
parka
peacock
pedestrian
persist
pike
pinto
pitchfork
plankton
pledge
ponder
probable
quenched
raven
recommend
rectangle

reliable
relish
remedy
retrieve
revive
rotate
saddlebag
salary
sandal
satin
sheriff
skateboard
sling
sluggish
specialist
stadium
starfish
strategy
streetcar
submarine
thermometer
tollbooth
torpedo
tote
triangle
tropical
twine
UFO
varmint
vehicle
veterinarian
wed
wrench
zookeeper

Grade 7

acid
actress
appliance
assist
backpack
bunt
cancel
carnation
chum
converse
decade
depot
earring
ecstatic
employer
famine
frequency
hairbrush
identical
ketchup
oval
participant
prescribe
touchdown
tumbleweed

Grade 8

alfalfa
crooked
despise
earnings
expansion
fertilizer
graveyard
lifeguard
living room

perishable
persuasive
replacement
shoulder high
toaster
yacht

Harris, Albert J., and Jacobson, Milton D. *Basic Reading Vocabularies.* New York: Macmillan Publishing Company, Inc.